Art Education

Art Education

HOWARD CONANT

Chairman, Department of Art Education
New York University

The Center for Applied Research in Education, Inc.
Washington, D.C.

LIBRARY OF CONGRESS
CATALOG CARD NO.: 64-11019

PRINTED IN THE UNITED STATES OF AMERICA

Foreword

Art Education as presented by Howard Conant is seen broadly. He includes a wealth of specific detail on teaching art as we know it in the United States, but he is not bogged down by a worm's-eye view of his subject.

Professional people of our day tend to create specialized categories of academic activities by processes of subdivision. Some of this kind of empire building in reverse has encouraged teachers to believe that art in the schools is primarily beneficial in achieving personal and/or social adjustment. Another view holds that art is important chiefly as an agent for the discovery and strengthening of the general creative urge.

Conant does not minimize art study as contributing to the above views, but his major emphasis, his point of departure, is clear in the titles of his first two chapters, "The Nature of Art" and "The Role of Art in Human Life."

"The Nature of Art" discusses "elements of quality in the art experience" and "personal characteristics which contribute to artistic creativity" are especially valuable to the general reader. While his elaboration of these categories can be comprehended in terms of other arts such as literature, or could be considered in relation to the sciences, he is careful to make his points particularly in relation to the visual and plastic arts. He is preoccupied with the unique qualities of art experience, of art expression, of the work of art.

As he sees it, the environment of the school must of necessity be one which provides experiences of aesthetic quality, both in opportunities for personal expression in painting, sculpture and design in many media, and in acquaintance with original works of arts. Anything less than this identifies a school as not doing all that it should for education in art.

The author's review of major emphases in art education makes valuable distinctions between the "laissez-faire," the "experimental," and the "child centered" approaches. He appraises the merits and the short comings of these limited objectives. His addition to these objectives of the terms "cultural context" and aesthetically oriented creative art teaching" express his conviction that education in art has a rightful place as an indispensable part of liberal education.

In "The Teaching of Art" he describes the kind of faculty and physical plant needed in art education if children are to have the best possible experiences. The catalog of needs is definite, clear, and thorough; it is not a vague generalization open to all manner of interpretation. The treatment of "Interest and Ability Levels in Art Education" is equally complete and useful.

His "Outlook for the Future of Art Education" is exciting, as it would have to be in view of the scope of what has gone before. Yet this concluding chapter is realistic. The most demanding requirements Conant makes on his colleagues in art education are already being met in scattered places. Art education can become what he urgently proposes, and his contribution in this volume is one which will hasten the day.

FREDERICK M. LOGAN
The University of Wisconsin

Art Education

Howard Conant

This volume on art education is an up-to-date, authoritative discussion of art in human living, art in the education of the individual, and the teaching of art. In this and other volumes on the teaching of science, language arts, health and safety, music, business subjects, and other areas, the Library of Education gives extensive coverage to the several fields of education.

The book emphasizes the importance and the nature of art, the historical development and philosophy of art education, teaching skills and practices at the several levels: in the home and nursery school, in the elementary, junior and senior high schools, in college and on through graduate study. The book is concluded with an interesting outlook for the future of art education.

The author is an articulate, competent, and most enthusiastic advocate of the importance and the significance of art education and creative art expression for all. He has documented this book with the findings of research where they are available and has given descriptions of sound practices.

WALTER A. ANDERSON
Content Editor

Contents

CHAPTER VII

CHAPTER I

The Nature of Art

To understand art, we must learn to see, to perceive, not merely look; and we must become *aware* of what we see and perceive. We must learn to feel, to respond emotionally; and we must be aware of such responses, not just vaguely motivated. To understand art we must learn to think visually, not just verbally; and we need to learn to respond empathetically (and, when possible, to respond physically) to works of art with which we come in contact.

Words cannot really explain art any more than they can explain music or the dance. The language of art is made up of such elements as texture and color and is based upon such principles as proportion and rhythm; but the meanings of the elements and principles of art are neither verbal nor constant: they are visual, and they vary in their application to specific art experiences and to particular works of art. In the language of art, color, for example, refers not to the word *color* or its verbal meaning but to a particular hue, of a particular degree of lightness or darkness and brightness or dullness, surrounded by other particular hues, and seen in a particular work of art created by a particular individual. The same particularity is characteristic of all the elements and principles of the language of art.

To understand the meaning of an art experience, one must, among other things, personally engage in such an experience. To begin to understand the meaning of a work of art, one must at some point be confronted by the actual work. Vicarious art experiences, reproductions, or verbal descriptions of works of art are poor substitutes.

There are, nevertheless, certain generalizations about art (not descriptions of art) which have been rather widely accepted by persons who have practiced or studied the subject, and these can serve as guides in helping us develop a basic understanding of the artistic process and the aesthetic qualities which underlie it. To this

1

fundamental knowledge we can subsequently add deeper, more personal, and specific (but nonverbal) elements of meaning which may, hopefully, enable us to enter the rarified, incredibly beautiful, and inexplicably profound realm of genuine aesthetic understanding.

The Art Experience

Two basic characteristics, *uniqueness* and *quality*, underlie the art experience and the works of art which are products of such experience. Each of these, of itself, is a desirable element of ordinary human experience; but both must be operative in an art experience. The uniqueness in an art experience is more or less synonymous with newness, originality, or creativeness. The *quality* of an art experience refers to its aesthetic significance, to the result of man's finest and most successful efforts in such fields as painting, sculpture, and architecture.

Uniqueness is often mistakenly equated with art experience. But art experience is much more than a "different" or "new" way of doing, making, seeing, or understanding something. An art experience is not only unique or new; it must also be superb. The art experience is one of the finest of which man is capable. In one sense, its results are more tangible than those of other high-level experiences; more often than not, an art experience produces a painting, a work of sculpture, or a building which enters the public domain and is subject to professional criticism. On the other hand, the experience of studying a work of art produced by someone else is much less tangible and is difficult to evaluate. But even an art experience which produces no tangible results may, nevertheless, have profound and noticeable effects—on behavior, attitudes, and beliefs.

It is difficult to state more clearly what is meant by uniqueness and quality in an art experience. Most artists and teachers of art refrain from making specific definitions because they recognize the complexity of the art experience and the danger of oversimplification. But since many persons who are not artists or art teachers wish to know more about this type of experience, and since many of them will affect the art experiences, art products, and art understandings of others, it is necessary to offer more information concerning these characteristics of the experience occasioned by the genesis, production, and study of works of art.

The character of uniqueness in the art experience. Complete uniqueness or total originality in the production of a work of art or in the experience gained in contemplating works of art is probably impossible to attain. Concerning this, Kris has said:

> ... art is not produced in an empty space, ... no artist is independent of predecessors and models, ... he no less than the scientist and philosopher is part of a specific tradition and works in a structured area of problems.[1]

The person engaged in the production or study of a work of art is deeply influenced by what he has seen, felt, and done throughout his life. On occasion, he will imitate to some degree—perhaps inadvertently—what he has seen or felt in the works of others.

Individuals utilizing certain types of art expression are, in varying degrees, imitating subject matter even if they interpret it in impressionistic or semiabstract styles. Even works of art which appear to be completely abstract are often highly refined interpretations of identifiable subject matter; and who is to say that even Mondrian, Pollock, Kline, and Albers were not significantly influenced by objects they saw and felt during their lives? Children and adults as well are deeply influenced by works of art they have seen in museums, galleries, books, and magazines. These influences are frequently and often clearly manifested in their work. The notion that imitation is deplorable, even harmful, is only one of a number of inherited art educational concepts which must be re-examined. Throughout history, artists have freely borrowed the techniques, the styles, and even the subject matter of others, usually taking care to give credit to the appropriate source.

Picasso, for example, created a series of paintings based on Delacroix's *Women of Algiers*. These, together with a color reproduction of the Delacroix, were exhibited at the Museum of Modern Art in New York. But neither Picasso's direct borrowing of certain elements of Delacroix's subject matter, composition, color, pattern, and texture, nor the exhibition in a major art museum of these variations on the theme of another artist, was openly criticized by art educators who, in their classrooms, often condemn copying, borrowing, and imitating. What confusion Picasso's Delacroix series

---

[1] Ernst Kris, *Psychoanalytic Explorations in Art* (New York: International Universities Press, Inc., 1952). Quoted in E. H. Gombrich, *Art and Illusion* (New York: Pantheon Books, Inc., 1960), p. 30.

would create in the mind of a bright pupil whose art teacher had decried imitation! Only rarely, however, do imitations of other artists' works attain the status of major paintings or sculptures. But who is to deny that the aesthetic significance of an artist's major works may not be due, in part, to the influence of others' works? Few artists and even fewer art teachers would advocate copying, or even borrowing, as the preferred way to develop artistic expressive powers. But it would seem that no one who has studied the history of art and modern theories of perception and art education should prohibit, either by edict or attitude, ways of learning (such as imitation or "interpretation" of the works of others) which have not been proved undesirable.

The uniqueness in an art experience, and the work of art or the understanding which grows out of such an experience, might be described as the feeling of freshness and oneness—a feeling which is to some extent new or original and quite different, though perhaps never wholly so, from other feelings one has had. One can experience uniqueness through the variation of a single line, a shape, a color, or a texture which may have appeared in slightly different form in an earlier work or in the work of another artist. Even the tiniest variation can cause an art experience and the work it produces to be regarded as either superior or inferior to one which is similar in every other respect.

Some elements of quality in the art experience. The quality of an art experience is even more difficult to explain. Much has been written about the quality of the art experience and many criteria for its evaluation have been suggested. Yet in nearly every case, when the writers have set forth their criteria, they conclude with the view that an unknown "something extra" must be provided by the artist or by the person who studies a work of art if the experience is to possess the quality of art. Faure, Camus, and many others have referred to the "leap" or "journey" one must take, unaccompanied, into the realm of aesthetic significance after one has mastered the elements of which it is believed to be composed. Expressed another way, it would seem the view of the most respected art theoreticians that the quality of an art experience or work of art is greater than the sum of its various components.

Not even the presence of all the known or presumed elements of quality in an art experience can assure the attainment of aesthetic significance; the "something extra" or the "leap" is necessary to bring these elements into a meaningful relationship. Bearing this in mind, let us separately consider each element in order to arrive at a better understanding of the structure of the qualitative aspect of art experience.

The elements of quality in the art experience have not been, and are perhaps not likely to be, clearly identified. Those which follow represent a subjective analysis based on studies of creativity which have been made by Guilford,[2] MacKinnon,[3] and others.

Certain elements of quality in the art experience are similar to those believed to exist in the works of art which are the tangible products of such experience. The most important elements in an art experience would appear to be those which tend to separate or differentiate it from experiences which are ordinary, meaningless, or negative. These elements include:

Selectiveness:	Isolating that which is essential and significant.
Transcendence:	Going beyond what is—or appears to be—seen, heard, felt, believed.
Truthfulness:	Striving for honesty, sincerity, and artistic worth.
Profoundness:	Seeking insight without loss of breadth; penetrating beneath surface qualities.
Intensity:	Sharpening focus on essentials; desiring involvement in what is seen or felt.
Gracefulness:	Seeking freedom from awkardness, shrillness, or overinsistence; preferring subtlety and interpretation to mere portrayal; desiring to be free of strain, artistically beautiful, moving, even poignant.
Emphasis:	Stressing aspects which appear artistically important.
Balance:	Countering one aspect with another, although seldom on an equivalent basis.
Proportion:	Giving unequal but well-related emphasis to various elements.
Rhythm:	Sensing, reacting, and expressing in periodic sequences.

---

[2] J. P. Guilford, "The Psychology of Creativity," *Creative Crafts,* n.d.

[3] Reported in "Creativity," Carnegie Corporation of New York *Quarterly* (July, 1961), 2–5.

Consistency: Striving for relatedness without succumbing
                      to excessive organization or overattention to
                      detail.

Comprehensiveness: Giving attention to coverage without com-
                      pulsive thoroughness.

Unity: Seeking order and harmony without loss of
                      variety.

Personal characteristics which contribute to artistic creativity.
Much has been written about the creative process. What many art
teachers have long sensed about creative expression has suddenly
become a matter of widespread interest with applications in nearly
every field of human endeavor. The concern here is to identify those
characteristics which go beyond mere creativity into the realm of
significant art expression, those which embrace both the unique (or
creative) and qualitative aspects of the art experience.

Every person can be said to possess, in varying degrees, the characteristic listed below.[4] Some individuals excel in many of these
characteristics; such persons would seem to have an unusually high
potential for significant art experiences. Other people may excel in
several of these characteristics but show only minimal aptitude or
ability in others; such individuals are believed to have a fair potential
for significant art experiences. Another group, probably the largest,
show only minimal aptitude or ability in these characteristics; such
people are believed to have little more than minimal potential for
significant art experiences. But since it is known that an intensive
program of art education can have a marked effect upon the development of many of these and other characteristics in nearly all individuals, it should not be assumed that the extent to which a person
possesses these qualities is exclusively a matter of inheritance or
native talent. Concerning this, Guilford has said:

> Aptitudes, including those most crucial to creative thinking, are
> thought to be determined both by heredity and by learning. Al-
> though heredity may set the ceiling above which the individual can-

---

[4] Summarizing the views of several researchers, W. Lambert Brittain reports:
"There seems to be a general opinion today that creative ability is distributed about
the population in a normal way, and everyone has at least some capacity to be
creative.... The creative person, then, is not unlike any of us except in degree."
In "An Experiment Toward Measuring Creativity," *Research in Art Education*,
Seventh Yearbook of the National Art Education Association (Kutztown, Pa.: The
Association,1956), p. 41.

not develop under the most favorable circumstances of life, it can be safely said that rarely does any individual reach his ceiling.[5]

In presenting a list of characteristics which are believed to contribute to artistic creativity, we have purposely begun with two which are popularly, and probably wrongly, believed to be the sole determinants of an individual's potential in this area.

Heredity. As Guilford and others have indicated, heredity is believed, though not known, to be an important factor in the art experience, more so at the uppermost reaches of significance than at the preliminary levels through which most individuals have to progress. It would be more fruitful to recognize the great artistic potential present in most individuals through excellent programs of art education than to expect the artistic giftedness of a parent to be reflected in the art experiences of a child.

Talent. Expressive talent and aesthetic insight, both of which are elements of the art experience and may, in part, be inherited, are believed to be characteristic of our most renowned artists. But no one is really sure of the meanings of these terms. Talent in sensing, in studying, and sometimes in solving art problems is probably best described by the characteristics which follow. The artistically talented or gifted person probably excels in many of them.

Since most young children show amazingly high degrees of ability in art expression and aesthetic comprehension, and since most of them appear to lose these abilities (perhaps because of negative influences in school and at home) during later childhood, the appellations of artistic talent, giftedness, or mature aesthetic sensitivity are usually reserved for adolescents or adults whose creative or aesthetic potential, as evidenced by works produced or by their understanding of the visual arts, is believed to be extremely high.

Aesthetic awareness. The artistically creative individual is usually sensitive to aesthetic qualities in all forms of expression. He is easily, often, and deeply motivated by a wide variety of stimuli. His aesthetic "perceptors" are always in action. Emotional responses are often more important to him than their more tangible, popularly observed aspects. He sees artistic form in films, in literature, in drama, in music, and in the dance, as well as in the particular area in which he works. He sees aesthetic qualities in nature, in human

---

[5] Guilford, *op. cit.*, p. 3.

beings, in engineering feats, in public events, and even in inartistic manmade objects in which such qualities are secondary and unplanned.

Perceptiveness.   The person capable of a high level of artistic creativity has a keen visual awareness: he sees things rather than merely looks at them. He sees them in detail; he senses their meanings and evaluates them. He has insight—both in flashes and over long periods of time. He senses relationships; he searches for valuable aesthetic qualities and finds them even in seeming absurdities.

Inventiveness.   Although his procedures may vary from those of the scientific inventor, the artistically creative individual is similar in many respects to innovators in other walks of life. He is forward-looking, ahead of his time, free from stereotyped patterns of thought and action, willing to take risks, and highly original. He can rapidly assimilate noteworthy accomplishments in the works of others without directly imitating them.

Flexibility.   The ability to adjust his reaction to given stimuli is characteristic of the artistically creative individual. He is not easily frustrated by variations in the appearance of things, in the attitudes of others, or in the progress of human events. Often he will capitalize on change and grasp in a moment the values inherent in an unexpected situation. Perhaps because of the endless changes encountered in his own working processes, the artistically creative person is often amazingly flexible.

Fluency.   Initial concepts are easily and rapidly enlarged, elaborated, or deepened, and successive steps in the working process are quickly sensed and expressed by the artistically creative person. (Guilford describes *fluency* as "ideas per minute.") Though he is seldom able to offer popularly understandable explanations of his work, it is laden with meaning and detailed information which can be perceived by the art-educated person.

Intelligence. In its broadest meaning, intelligence contributes to (and indeed may be used to describe collectively) the characteristics which are believed to contribute to significance in the art experience. But in the narrower definition of intelligence (once believed to be measurable by paper-and-pencil tests)—even in the definition of intelligence as a mental or fact-gathering capacity—there is no evidence to prove its positive correlation with an individual's artistic or aesthetic potential. Most artistically and aesthetically gifted adolescents and adults are intelligent; they are "bright," thoughtful, reflective, analytic, and able to synthesize data. They usually have good memories (more often for broad concepts than for minor details) which, in artistic matters, function as "data-processing machines." Intelligence would seem to contribute to the art experience, but research to date has not indicated in what ways these human attributes are related.[6]

Independence.　A high degree of individualism (nonconformism at its best) and a sense of "conscientious revolt," appear essential to significance in the art experience. The artistically creative person needs and wants to develop his own ideas, to be free of restrictive conventions. He is often impulsive, self-assertive, determined—even aggressive, stubborn, or bold. On occasion he requires what Margaret Mead calls "aloneness." He is usually confident of his own ability, but he is self-critical and applies the most rigorous of personal standards to his work. To "outsiders," many of them well-meaning but sometimes unintentionally restrictive parents and teachers, the artistically creative individual often appears to be eccentric, uncouth, brazen, vain, and aloof. He is not "well-rounded" (MacKinnon says creative persons have "sharp edges"); he may even be neurotic.[7]

Integrity.　Although he is often regarded skeptically by laymen, the artistically creative person is probably one of the most honest of people. To him, sincerity in his concepts, working processes, and products, are of paramount importance. His work, and his attitude toward it, are moral in the very highest sense. He places artistic and aesthetic (which are akin to spiritual) values above material ones.

---

[6] Studies conducted by E. Paul Torrance of the University of Minnesota's Bureau of Educational Research suggest that outstanding creativity is seldom found among children of below-average IQ, but that, on the other hand, IQ's above 115 or 120 have no apparent bearing on creativity. He concludes that normally intelligent children's potential for achievement in school and in life is therefore not limited by their IQ scores, and that, in fact, children with high IQs may develop memory and logical reasoning powers at the expense of insight, imagination, and adventurousness—qualities he believes are essential to genius. Reported in "Some Implications for Art Education," from the Minnesota Studies of Creative Thinking, *Studies in Art Education* (Washington, D.C.: National Art Education Association, Spring, 1961), pp. 36–43; and in John K. Lagemann, "How We Discourage Creative Children," *Redbook* (March, 1963), 44, 45.

[7] Concerning this quality popularly believed to be characteristic of artists (Van Gogh and others being cited as examples), Guilford has said: "The creative person is not necessarily neurotic or psychotic. In fact, there is evidence that being neurotic is a handicap." *Op. cit.,* p. 3.

He is deeply concerned with human problems. The artistically creative person often deals openly and forcefully with concepts which to him seem important, regardless of public opinion.

Gregariousness. Although a high degree of artistic creativity is not usually manifested as a personal characteristic until adolescence, it is possible that the person who possesses it might display, even as a child, the clannish qualities exemplified by most artists. Though the person who is frequently engaged in significant art experiences seeks an undisturbed working place, he usually finds association with artistically inclined people stimulating.

Efficiency. The artistically creative person is efficient, but in his own, often uncommon, way. His life and working habits are ordered and planned, but they vary greatly from one individual to another. The nine-to-five routine characteristic of the businessman may be unworkable for the artistically creative individual. He may choose to work from, say, five in the evening to three in the morning in order to have greater opportunity for undisturbed attention to his work, a practice which causes some persons to mistake his diligence for Bohemianism.

Involvement. In matters connected with his artistic endeavors, the creative person nearly always is deeply involved. As a rule, he has to be very patient. With little or no thought of time, monetary rewards, the cost or amount of materials, sleep, or even food, he usually works carefully, giving unlimited attention to details he considers important and reworking anything which is not quite right. For the professional artist, "rightness" may not occur for a month, a year, a decade, or even longer—yet he works patiently and arduously toward that goal. Unlike many persons, the artistically creative individual is less eager to finish a work or to complete a certain number of works in a given period of time than he is to attain aesthetic significance. In his art experiences, he can tolerate failure, ambiguity, lack of critical or public recognition, complexity, and a working environment which to the layman might seem impossible. He can delay self-criticism to avoid nipping in the bud ideas which might eventually prove worthwhile.

High output. A high level of productivity on the part of an artistically creative person greatly enhances the opportunity for significant art experiences and resultant works of excellence to emerge. The artictically creative person applies himself to his work with energy, vigor, and enthusiasm—even to the extent of seeming to neglect normal social relationships. He is deeply involved in his work, yet at times he may—while thinking—appear to be doing nothing (which is one reason for his need for isolation). At other times he may work actively for days on end. Output varies greatly among artistically creative individuals, since some put much effort and time into a few works while others rapidly produce numerous works. But in both cases a nearly continuous outpouring of creative energy usually proves fruitful in the production of works of aesthetic significance.

It is worthwhile to note a similarity between this list of characteristics which are believed to contribute to artistic creativity and a summary of professional opinion on the characteristics of the generally creative person. Such a person is pictured as one who

> . . . would have rich experiences; that is, he would interact freely with his environment though his life on the surface may appear no more "romantic" than any other. He can use his experiences in new situations, is quick to see relationships, and can assemble many pertinent ideas to focus upon a problem. He is flexible in his approach to new ideas, and can easily handle numerous thoughts at once. He has an abundance of energy which he voluntarily uses to alter displeasing situations and to invent, write, paint, or otherwise produce. He has a certain sensitivity to his environment, seeing differences and similarities where others miss them. He can think abstractly and his thoughts are often unusual or novel; sometimes he seems intuitive and has insight into problems or situations. He is usually a well-adjusted and happy person.[8]

J. P. Guilford surveyed "the known primary traits that are believed to be related to creativity" and identified the following aptitudes for creative thinking: sensitivity to problems, fluency of thinking, flexibility, originality, redefinition, and elaboration. Among the nonaptitude traits related to creativity cited by Guilford are: "willingness to work hard and to work long hours," "a very high level of general motivation," "tolerance of ambiguity," "convergent thinking," "divergent thinking," "need for adventure," an inclination "to be more impulsive, more ascendant, and more confident and to have a stronger appreciation of creativity," an inclination "to appreciate aesthetic expression, and to like reflective thinking," a

---

[8] Brittain, *op. cit.,* p. 41.

tendency "to be more confident," and "a strong need for variety." [9]

In a recent summary of research on teaching the visual arts, Hausman cited three studies which are also pertinent to the foregoing list of characteristics which are believed to contribute to artistic creativity:

> Beittel and Lowenfeld (1959) compared a listing of attributes identified in their own study with factors identified by Guilford 1950, 1954). Terms such as *flexibility, closure, originality, sensitivity,* and *fluency* were common to both of the lists.
>
> Maslow (1957, 1959) has projected what happens to cognition when it is involved in creative experience: the personality fuses into a fully functioning, idiosyncratic whole. He postulates that a person involved in creative activity experiences in a unified manner—a manner in which dichotomies, polarities, contradictions, and conflicts tend to fuse. Through such involvement, perception becomes richer and more sensitive. . . . As such, cognition acquires a special flavor of wonder, of awe, and of humility before one's creative powers.
>
> Mooney (1953) . . . identified four "dimensions" for describing and accounting for creativity: (1) openness to the reception and extension of experience; (2) focusing of experience: movement toward differentiation and realization of self; (3) disciplined management and aesthetic forming; and (4) deriving significance from experience. [10]

Instructional procedures and environmental conditions which may enhance significance in the art experience. Although the artistically creative person is often self-directed, certain instructional procedures and environmental conditions are believed to enhance the significance of his art experiences.

Instruction. A skillful, creative, sincere, and patient teacher, parent, or peer, is (except for the individual himself) the most important means of enhancing the significance of an art experience. Stimulation, nonindoctrinary instruction, continued encouragement, and constructive criticism are of inestimable value to the child, adolescent, or adult who is to engage in artistic creativity at a high level of aesthetic significance. Unfortunately, teachers, parents, and

---

[9] Guilford, "Traits of Creativity," in *Creativity and Its Cultivation,* edited by Harold H. Anderson (New York: Harper & Row, Publishers, 1959), pp. 144–57.

[10] Jerome Hausman, "Research on Teaching the Visual Arts," in *Handbook on Research of Teaching,* edited by N. L. Gage (Chicago: Rand McNally & Co., 1963), pp. 1107, 1108.

peers who can provide such help are rare. As Gardner Murphy
has said:

> We know relatively little about how to encourage, but all too
> much about how to impede. We find a thousand devices for regular-
> izing, stabilizing, restraining, or even poking fun at the earliest ex-
> ploratory efforts of children.[11]

Stimuli. Artistic creativity in various individuals can be initiated by every conceivable type of stimulus, ranging from the mere
provision of materials and time to the introduction of powerful
ideological concepts. In most cases, daily experiences, clarified and
enriched by a skillful parent or teacher, serve adequately as stimuli
for the child's artistic creativity. Adolescents, adults, and—to an
even greater extent—professional artists, usually require more complex and more deeply effective forms of motivation. Although in
some cases these can be self-induced, external stimuli provided by
teachers, peers, nature, manmade objects, and external events often
provide stronger motivational forces. It is, however, no longer believed that certain stimuli are best suited for a particular chronological age or grade level. The interests and abilities of individuals
at any age level range widely, and the most effective stimulus for
artistic creativity is usually one which is well-suited for, and directed
toward, a particular individual. This fact automatically renders
second-best those educational situations with high pupil-teacher
ratios, in which individual motivation becomes a chance occurence.

Environment. Although individuals are capable of significant
art experiences in seemingly impossible situations, certain environmental conditions are known to be more conducive to such experiences. Ideally, the atmosphere should be pleasant and reasonably
quiet. The person engaged in creative activity should not be hur-
ried or interrupted; he should be provided with necessary materials
and a satisfactory place to work and he should be allowed to work
alone or with persons of his own choice. There should be an easy
give-and-take relationship with parents, teachers, or peers.

Extremely important for the artistically creative individual, as
well as for the society of which he is a part, is the general attitude
of society toward creativity in general and artistic giftedness in particular. As Toynbee has eloquently said:

---

[11] Gardner Murphy, "The Process of Creative Thinking," *Educational Leadership* (October, 1956), 11–14.

... to give a fair chance to potential creativity is a matter of life and death for any society.... outstanding creative ability... is mankind's ultimate capital asset, and the only one with which Man has been endowed.... children are even more sensitive to hostile public opinion than adults are, and are even readier to purchase, at almost any price, the toleration that is an egalitarian-minded society's alluring reward for poor-spirited conformity.[12]

The developmental process in artistic creativity. The following description represents a general consensus of the nature of the developmental process in artistic creativity.

Initial conception. The initial phase of artistic creativity varies greatly among individuals. Most persons first conceive of an idea and then develop it in an art form. Their initial conception appears to range from sudden flashes of insight or inspiration to (according to Guilford) a gradual perception of related ideological and/or pictorial elements:

> Many ideas, unlike hothouse plants, cannot be forced into bloom.... Come back to it again and again (it will also come back spontaneously, perhaps with a new idea each time). The time will come when the whole solution will almost unfold before you.[13]

But certain artists say that they approach a bare canvas or block of wood, pick up a brush, pencil, or tool, and simply begin to work. Their first colors, lines, or shapes "suggest" others. At times the first few shapes or lines applied by the creative individual may be the complete work. The work may seem to have sprung from the artist's brush to the canvas (as, for example, some works by Picasso). Clearly, this "initial" stage (which may, indeed, have been preceded by years of thought and/or practice) does not fit into a definition of the initial phase of artistic creativity as a gradual unfolding which cannot be confined to one sitting.

Conceptual refinement. The artistically creative individual often reflects upon his initial conception, considers variations, and evaluates their artistic and ideological worth. As a result, he may either proceed to successive phases of the creative process, alter the original conception, or abandon the idea and choose another.

Selection of medium and mode of expression. Once the con-

---

[12] Arnold Toynbee, "U.S. Stifles Creativity," *New York University Alumni News* (January, 1962), p. 3.

[13] Guilford, "The Psychology of Creativity," *op. cit.*, p. 3.

ception has been crystallized (or, in the case of persons who appear to experience both phases simultaneously, during the conception/ refinement period), the artistically creative person selects the medium and the mode of expression he feels are best suited to the implementation of his idea. Although he may—and quite often does —change his mind later, at this point he will probably decide on the medium (oil paint, watercolor, gouache, pencil), the support (canvas, paper, cardboard, wood), and the mode or style of expression (geometric abstraction, realism, abstract expressionism, impressionism) which he feels are likely to enhance his conception and make it possible for him to produce a work of the highest quality of which he is capable. Most artistically creative people, however, do not so much choose a mode or style of expression as gradually develop one. Usually, they work in the same mode or style over a period of time, perhaps gradually varying or refining it. Very rarely (if their work is of aesthetic significance) do they switch abruptly from one style to another.

Production of the work.   The amount of inspiration, thought, and reflection which precedes the actual production of a work of art appears to range from none (according to artists who claim this process evolves simultaneously with production) to very much. But in nearly all cases artistically creative people continue refining their initial concept throughout the period of production. Again, there is a vast range in the amount of refinement. Some artists proceed, with what would almost seem to be inartistic matter-of-factness, to execute their conceptions in a highly ordered step-by-step fashion. Others experience great difficulties, cannot make up their minds, appear to vacillate or even to reverse themselves, and may only after great effort produce a work which satisfies them. But both they and more orderly creative individuals will go so far as to destroy works with which they are displeased.

There are as many working procedures as there are creative individuals to develop them, and each work calls for new techniques and solutions. Contrary to the theories expounded in popular how-to-do-it books, there is no "right" or "wrong" way to produce a work of art. In fact, much evidence exists to indicate that following someone else's step-by-step suggestions is an almost certain guarantee of artistic failure.

Artistically creative persons strive to bring their works to a state

of "rightness" which, for the moment at least, is reasonably satisfying to them. But it is not at all unusual for them to rework a piece
which they had earlier felt to be "right."

Conception of additional works.   We have seen that neither the
conception of works of art nor their production is an isolated, orderly process. Similarly, the conception of additional works seldom
follows immediately upon the completion of a given work. New
works are frequently conceived, often begun, and sometimes even
completed, during the production of a work which had been started
earlier. Working in what seems to be a disordered fashion is essential to most artistically creative individuals. Without the freedom
to work absolutely as they wish, at any time, for any length of time,
with any medium, in any size, and in their own way, both they and
their work appear to be hampered. To find means of providing
artistically creative children and adolescents, even college students,
with the freedom required by the nature of the art experience is a
major educational problem.

Types of art experience.   A number of art educators and psychologists have made studies of individuals, their working processes,
and the works they have produced in an effort to determine various
types of art aptitudes or behavioral characteristics. By testing 1128
children for what he called "visual or haptic aptitude," Lowenfeld
found (in a study which enjoyed wide popularity among art educators during the decade following its publication) that "47 per
cent were clearly visual, 23 per cent were haptic, and 30 per cent
either received a score below the line where a clear identification
was possible, or were otherwise not identifiable." [13] Lowenfeld
found that the "visual starts from his environment, that he feels as
a spectator, and that his intermediaries for experience are mainly
the eyes. The other, . . . the haptic type, is primarily concerned with
his own body sensations and the subjective experiences in which he
feels emotionally involved." [14]

A more recent, less extensive, but nevertheless important study
by Gaitskell [15] indicated that children who produce works which
might, according to Lowenfeld's definitions, be classified as "visual,"

---

[13] Viktor Lowenfeld, *Creative and Mental Growth,* 3rd ed. (New York: The
MacMillan Company, 1957), p. 263.

[14] *Ibid.,* p. 262.

[15] C. D. Gaitskell, *Children and Their Art* (New York: Harcourt, Brace, &
World, Inc., 1958).

"haptic," or a combination of the two, can, through the efforts of a skillful teacher, be helped to conceive and produce works which are no longer classifiable only according to their original type.

Other studies claim the existence of many more aptitudes than the two described by Lowenfeld, but none has been sufficiently extensive or validated to warrant mention here. The consensus among leading art educators today is that each child is a type unto himself, and that although his art experience and creative works may, on occasion, resemble those of other children, educational emphasis should be placed upon the development of individual uniqueness rather than on the tabulation of similarities.

There is, however, one problem which must concern those who are interested in continuing improvements in art education. Quite simply, it is a matter of differentiating among juvenile, adolescent, adult, and professional art experiences in order to avoid confusion which can be harmful to members of each group as well as to the society as a whole (see Chapter IV). We have seen that the exact nature of the art experience at any age level is unknown and that it will probably remain so. But on the other hand, we do have enough information about it (see Bibliography, p. 109) to make some fairly reliable generalizations.

Early childhood art experiences. The fact that children are capable of art experience prior to the age of one has been proven by some rather striking drawings, paintings, and models produced by nine-month-old children. Early childhood art experiences are essentially free and uninhibited; they seem directly related to emotional and physical conditions. The child of one to three or four years of age does not draw or paint what he sees in the manner of an artist sketching a scene. Indeed, he may at times barely be conscious that he has expressed his feelings in the tangible form of art. As he gets older, his scribbled or free-form works indicate awareness of subject-matter elements. But, it is believed, he still creates from within, graphically expressing his total concepts of things rather than making a direct portrayal of their appearance.

Intermediate childhood art experiences. As the child's intellectual powers increase, his art experiences are profoundly influenced. His inner concepts—which have previously been affected as much by emotional responses, sounds, smells, and movements, as by appearance—are now increasingly affected by what he sees and comes to know intellectually about various objects, persons, and events. Though the conflicts among a child's original concept of an object, his first visual awareness of the object, and his gathering of intellectual information about it present him with a very complex problem, it is one which he can (with proper guidance from his teachers, parents, and peers) repeatedly solve without diminishing his artistic and aesthetic powers. Unfortunately, most children receive the wrong kind of guidance at this crucial time and their resultant inability to cope satisfactorily with the conflict between what they feel, see, and come to know is frequently fatal to artistic and aesthetic growth.

Adolescent art experiences. The teen-ager who is fortunate enough to resolve the childhood conflict among the conceptual, emotional, visual, and intellectual aspects of his art experiences is capable of intense art expression and profound aesthetic judgment. His boundless energy, awakening impulses, greater intellectual maturity, and powerful emotional responses make him capable of highly significant art experiences. Most youngsters, however, receiving inadequate art educational guidance during this period, resort to trivial modes of expression and have difficulty with aesthetic concepts.

Adult art experiences. Millions of adults are participating in an unprecedented surge of nonprofessional art activity. Today's abundance of adult education courses, do-it-yourself books, clubs, and television programs, together with the recommendations and guidance of friends, make it difficult for the layman *not* to "learn to paint" and to "understand" art. Unfortunately, sound art educational practices do not prevail in the opportunities most easily available to interested adults, so that the resultant art experiences are frequently superficial.

Prodded by art materials and do-it-yourself art book manufacturers, and taught by instructors who may know better but who need the money and think it really doesn't matter if "mere amateurs" engage in basically inartistic endeavors, a really sizable segment of the adult population is being artistically and aesthetically hoodwinked. Not only are they led to believe they understand the meaning of art after a half-dozen round-table discussions led by a graduate of last term's class, but many adult participants in studio-type classes are encouraged, after the first few weeks, to exhibit their humble works and even to offer them for sale.

Nonprofessional, hobby-type art activity does, unquestionably, have therapeutic and social values, but these are hardly worth cultivating at the expense of individual and communal cultural integrity. In order to be valid and worthwhile, art educational programs for adult laymen should be as carefully constructed and skillfully guided as those in the finest secondary schools and colleges.

Professional art experiences. The "freedom from care and strife" to which Strauss referred in his "Artist's Life Waltz," is rarely applicable to serious and gifted professionals. Their art experiences could hardly involve more thoughtfulness, effort, and attention to detail, and they strive continually to produce better, more significant works. Even in his private life, the true professional artist's experiences are rarely free of care and strife. Of course, the seemingly carefree, Bohemian pseudo-artist made his presence as well known in the nineteenth century as he does at present, but this should not mislead us as it did Strauss.

The experiences of the serious professional artist (as differentiated from the commercial artist or the untalented painter or sculptor who somehow manages to exhibit and sell his work) are profound, intense, and usually interrelated. The artist's experiences are not pleasurable in the popular sense. They are sometimes painful, upsetting, saddening; but at other times they may be thrilling, evocative, physically uplifting, or spiritually moving. Such experiences are necessary to the serious professional artist: he could not produce works of aesthetic significance without them.

The Work of Art

The popular expression "I don't know anything about art, but I know what I like" contains more meaning than is usually intended. In a very important sense art is, indeed, what one "likes." But to like art, one must understand it and, unfortunately, few people do. What most people refer to as an example of what they "like" may only incidentally be a work of art. Art is much more than illustration or decoration, and to "like" a particular work for either of these qualities is, usually, to miss its aesthetic essence altogether. To "like" a particular work for its illustrative content or its decorative quality is similar to liking a person because of the way he dresses or because of the color of his hair. Although these may indeed be qualities worth admiring, they tell us comparatively little about the person's essential human qualities which should be our primary concern. The most important qualities in works of art are those which are profound, lasting, and unique—those which require effort, willingness, and time in order to be determined, understood, and appreciated.

Recent experiments in the art education of children indicate that sound aesthetic judgment may be an inherent human characteristic which, with adequate guidance, makes it possible for all people to develop a meaningful and lasting understanding of the arts. Some children's responses to questions such as "What is art?" and "What does art mean to you?" have been found to differ little, in essence, from those of knowledgeable art critics and scholars! Here, for example, are views expressed by eleven-year-old pupils of the Clear Stream Avenue Elementary School in Valley Stream, N.Y.:

> Art is a memory of vision.
> Art means to me the form of culture . . . the way a painter shows what he feels about life. . . .
> Sometimes . . . [artists] bring out ways people feel inside. Also, artists produce things they imagine, but they really *do* exist.

Art educators now have reason to believe that most adults' seeming lack of understanding of the arts may, instead, be suppressed understanding. They believe that certain well-intentioned but actually negative parental, educational, and environmental influences have caused many people to substitute nonaesthetic values for their inherent sensitivity to essential art qualities. Art educators are now attempting to build upon what they believe to be the child's awareness of fundamental art qualities in order that this aesthetic sensitivity may be carried over into adult life. The interested and willing individual can, if he will, independently develop an understanding of art's most essential qualities. The description which follows may enable the reader to grasp the essential meaning of art, approach an understanding of its totality, and eventually be affected by as many of its values as possible.

Art includes music, the dance, drama, and sometimes literature, as well as painting, sculpture, architecture, the graphic arts, and—

at its best—applied design. A work of art is a unique and superb product of human expression. But art is usually, and perhaps most appropriately, thought of in its tangible forms—painting, sculpture, and architecture—rather than in its intangible forms—concepts or experiences, natural phenomena, or manmade objects of mediocre aesthetic quality.

The uniqueness of a work of art is determined by the inventiveness and originality of the artist. The superb quality which outstanding works of art possess is a result of the artist's ability to employ and to orchestrate successfully the various elements and principles of art. The characteristics of uniqueness and quality in works of art distinguish such products of human endeavor from the many others which are mundane, stereotyped, imitative, or mediocre. The trained observer usually senses these characteristics in works of art through a combination of intuition, formal and independent study, direct observation of works of art, conversations with artists and other knowledgeable persons, and considerable reflection. The unsophisticated directness and perceptiveness of children often permits them to sense these characteristics on a probably less rational and intellectual but perhaps more lasting basis. To develop the important ability to sense uniqueness and quality in works of art, the adult apparently needs to learn all he can about the subject, see as many original works of art as possible, discuss them with other persons, reflect thoughtfully, and then proceed from mere familiarity with the elements and principles of art to an independent, total aesthetic judgment.

Somewhere in the makeup and functions of their body-mind-spirit totality, artists from earliest times have apparently understood aesthetic qualities and have developed enough artistic skill to produce works of great importance. And just as some persons possess a native talent for producing works of art, so do others appear to have an intuitive ability to grasp the aesthetic essence of these works. It is now believed that the ability necessary for both the production and understanding of works of art can be appreciably developed through programs of art education and aesthetically rich environments:

> The reorganization of our visual habits, so that we perceive not isolated "things" in "space," but structure, order, and the relatedness of events in space-time is perhaps the most profound kind of

revolution possible—a revolution that is long overdue not only in art, but in all our experience.[16]

Superb quality in a work of art, though only rarely achieved, is believed to be attained by the "right" combination (unique to each work) of elements and by the implementation of certain artistic principles. Among the elements available to the artist are color, texture, line, space, and content (or subject matter). Among the principles by which he will probably (though often unconsciously) be guided are rhythm, emphasis, proportion, unity, variety, and the appropriateness of medium, technique, and style to content.

A work of art is highly, often powerfully, communicative. Its "message," however, is usually a combination of fact and feeling and is best communicated to persons who possess an inherent artistic sensitivity or acquired aesthetic knowledge—persons who are willing to permit art to affect them.

A work of art portrays the times in which it was produced; yet its portrayal is not literal or complete in the usual sense. Only rarely might it be called objective. When a work of art does "describe," it does so superbly—usually with overtones of psychology, fantasy, religion, or philosophy; it may be more a microscopic, telescopic, or dream-world image than a precise rendition of what appears to the naked eye.

Some works of art do not seem to portray or reflect the times in which they were produced. Joseph Wood Krutch, who believes this, has said:

> Anyone who turns from the contemplation of most European literature or any of the other arts to study the record of its social or political history will find it hard to believe that the art was created in such a world. What we know of life in the Middle Ages —even for the relatively privileged—seems to us to have been composed of perpetual discomfort and quick, recurring horrors. Yet even the fortresses built during the darkest of the Dark Ages are grimly beautiful. . . . Look at Chartres or any of the other cathedrals built as the Middle Ages came to an end.[17]

Yet even in Krutch's attempt to indicate a possible disparity between

---

[16] S. I. Hayakawa, in *Language of Vision*, edited by G. Kepes (Chicago: P. Theobald & Company, Pubs., 1944), p. 10.

[17] Joseph Wood Krutch, "Boost, Don't Knock," *Saturday Review* (December 16, 1961), 11.

works of art and the times in which they were produced, one senses a profound relatedness between *grimly beautiful* and *the darkest of the Dark Ages*. Art's subtle insight often conveys the essence of a period more forcefully than do detailed historical descriptions.

A work of art interprets rather than describes; it penetrates to the essence of the subject with which it deals, and though it is (as a rule) created by one person, it reflects the feelings of many men. The artist's portrayal of his times, particularly when rendered in the newer modes of abstract expression, may not be recognized as such during his own lifetime except by the most perceptive of critics. The cultural lag between popular understanding and contemporary artistic achievement has always been considerably wide; but many of today's less easily communicative artistic forms are proving even more difficult for the public to assimilate.

Works of art range, in their tangible forms, from small, quickly executed pencil sketches to huge, slowly developed murals; from tiny clay models to massive marble sculptures; from simple, private homes to major commercial or governmental buildings.

Only rarely do objects of jewelry, ceramics, furniture, clothing, or industrial design which have been created by men, or by machines designed by men, attain the level of quality known as art. There are many reasons for the aesthetic weakness of most objects in these categories, but chief among them, undoubtedly, is the fact that the maker's primary consideration is producing a quickly salable object, rather than attaining uniqueness and superb quality.

The time taken to produce a work of art, its size, the technical complexity of its execution, its monetary value, its degree of realism, and the private life of its creator, though interesting, are not regarded as valid criteria for the determination of aesthetic significance. A small charcoal drawing by a comparatively unknown artist may be far superior, aesthetically, to a large, expensive oil painting by an artist of international renown. One of the great and lasting pleasures of mature aesthetic judgment is the ability to recognize works of outstanding quality among those produced by lesser-known artists.

The appearance, size, media, location, use, monetary value, and popularity of works of art have varied greatly over the centuries, yet all works which are generally regarded as being of aesthetic importance possess in common the fundamental attributes of uniqueness and superbly high quality. It is quite possible to denote—even to compare—these attributes in works of art which differ widely in date and place of origin, medium, size, intended use, and acceptance by the public.

Summary

Though art cannot specifically be defined, certain generalizations concerning its nature are useful in bringing the learner to the threshold of aesthetic understanding and artistically significant expression. By developing familiarity with the characteristics of uniqueness and qualitative excellence—in both the creation and the study of works of art—the learner will be able, through subsequent personal initiative, to understand the meanings of various art forms and to express himself creatively at an increasingly higher level of aesthetic significance. He will thus be able to benefit more fully from art's many values.

CHAPTER II

The Role of Art in Human Life

Art is richly laden with potential benefits for individuals as well as for the society of which they are a part. The values of art are at least as important, and probably as numerous, as the values of science and technology. But because art has been grossly neglected by state and federal governments, by educational systems, and by individuals themselves, its many life-enriching values have not affected more than a relatively few people.

Science and technology have made our lives safer, increased our leisure, and rendered mass communications and travel both quicker and easier. These popularly enjoyed benefits have been made possible by generous governmental, educational, and private philanthropic support. But what kind of individual and social life have the widely shared and generously supported benefits of science and technology provided? How do we use our increased leisure time? Where is the beauty in our homes and communities? Is it not true, as Herbert Read has said:

> Our particular trouble, in this "air-conditioned nightmare" which we call a civilization, is that we have lost the very notion of cultivating the senses, until butterfingered and tongue-tied, half-blind and deaf to all nervous vibrations, we stumble through life unaware of its most appealing aspects, lost to its intensest joys and communions.[1]

As Read and other highly perceptive social philosophers [2] have pointed out with frightening clarity, life that does not involve art is comparatively devoid of worthwhile meaning and purpose. Such a life is dangerous in many ways; it is not beautiful; it is actively unappealing; and it is humdrum in the most routine way imaginable. Life without art lacks excitement; it is unembellished, unenriched,

---

[1] Herbert Read, *The Grass Roots of Art* (New York: George Wittenborn, Inc., 1947), p. 37.
[2] Such as Lewis Mumford, Percival and Paul Goodman, and Richard Neutra.

unenlightened, and unexhilarating; it is not fully civilized and lacks the full, fresh consciousness of which human beings are supremely capable.

Unlike most of mankind's highly prized commodities, the arts are, for the most part, freely accessible to all persons or societies who will but accept them. Without having to be asked and without being guaranteed financial reward, security, or prestige, artists continue to create the very finest works of which they are capable and strive to make them available to everyone.

Although the fundamental aesthetic qualities of the arts have remained more or less constant throughout the ages, artists today are possibly more conscious of the potential human values of their work than their predecessors were. No doubt the critical nature of modern individual and social life has caused the artist to desire, more strongly than before, a widespread implementation of the life-giving, civilizing, and beautifying values inherent in works of art.

From the earliest of times, artists have served both as prophets and as portrayers of human life. In their cave paintings of animals and hunters, prehistoric artists illustrated important aspects of the dominant interests of their times and provided a measure of spiritual strength for their fellow men. It is likely that the members of early societies who observed these works of art gained not only a better understanding of their personal interests and beliefs and increased courage to face the dangers of everyday life but also aesthetic pleasure as well. Today, the works of prehistoric artists are looked upon as outstanding examples of artistic accomplishment, particularly in the way they capture the essence of their subject matter and in their beauty of line and shape, graceful rhythm, subtly related colors, and cohesive composition.

Later artists continued to depict, interpret, and prophesy the activities, interests, and beliefs of their fellow men. Several thousand years before the birth of Christ, Egyptian artists, working under the strictest imaginable canons of artistic style and with their choice of subject matter rigidly limited, produced works of superb aesthetic quality which formed a core of excellence in the culture of that period. We realize today that, in spite of the restrictions which a society may impose upon its artists, inventive minds must and will find ways of communicating with artistically sensitive persons. One cannot help wondering how significant to the lives of Egyptians were their artists' slight deviations from priestly edicts governing artistic style and subject matter choice.

During the Greek and Roman eras, as well as in the Mycenaean, Assyrian, and Etruscan cultures, artists reached extremely high levels of aesthetic significance. Their works must have had a profound effect upon the nature of those ancient civilizations. The eventual dissolution of the Roman Empire was, incidentally, evident in the imitative, increasingly less significant, and comparatively lifeless forms of painting, sculpture, and architecture produced by artists during the last century of that era.

Art flourished again during the Gothic and Renaissance periods, when thousands of magnificent works of architecture, painting, and sculpture were produced. Large segments of the public were so deeply involved in, and affected by, the arts during these periods that philosophers, sociologists, and other enlightened persons have ever since striven to establish the arts in society on a similarly broad and fruitful basis.

In the seventeenth and eighteenth centuries, both art and the public fared less well. Art became a plaything of the very wealthy; it lost much of its vigor and integrity, and its aesthetic significance was subordinate to its decorative qualities. Artists catered to the emotional whims and social interests of the upper classes and virtually ignored the lay public. It is doubtful that even the aristocracy derived more than the most superficial aesthetic values from the painting, sculpture, and architecture of that time, although such artists as Boucher and Fragonard managed to attain comparatively high levels of artistic quality.

Just how large a segment of the public in each era benefits from the values inherent in the art of their own and earlier periods is not known. But we may assume that greater degrees of popular understanding existed when styles of expression were more realistic— when the subject matter, though perhaps not the underlying aesthetic aspects, of given works could be recognized and at least superficially understood by the average spectator.

A comparatively high level of popular communication was achieved by Goya, Daumier, Gericault, Delacroix, Manet, and other late eighteenth and nineteenth century artists. Their penetrating portrayals of ordinary people and contemporary events had a widespread effect upon the public of their time, providing both inspiration for and clarification of the complex problems of revolution and the rise of the common man.

The cultural lag between popular understanding and contemporary artistic accomplishment probably became most clearly apparent in the early twentieth century. As the work of leading artists became increasingly abstract, the public was (and still is) estranged from the essential values found in modern modes of artistic expression. It would seem that whatever public understanding of the arts had developed in earlier periods was primarily an appreciation of its subject matter, rather than of its fundamental aesthetic qualities. On the other hand, one might hopefully suppose that an intuitively or educationally enlightened minority must always have understood the aesthetic qualities which separate art from mere illustration. As the distinguished art historian, Arnold Hauser, has indicated:

> The way to a genuine appreciation of art is through education. Not the violent simplification of art, but the training of the capacity for aesthetic judgment is the means by which the constant monopolizing of art by a small minority can be prevented. . . . It will never be possible for everyone to enjoy and appreciate it in equal measure, but the share of the broader masses in it can be increased and deepened. The preconditions of a slackening of the cultural monopoly are above all economic and social. We can do no other than fight for the creation of these preconditions.[3]

A number of practical values can be enjoyed by persons who develop an understanding of the arts. Community planning at its finest affords better health, greater economy, and simpler, faster, and safer communication and mobility. And, as in the case of Brazil's new capital city, it can attain a level of colossal, deeply moving, artistic beauty. Architecture and interior design affect people profoundly, intimately, and extensively and are, of course, essential to the overall aesthetic quality of the community. Since all of us are deeply affected, positively or negatively, by every element in the enviroment, the need to provide ourselves with communities comprised of schools and other public buildings of the highest possible artistic merit is obvious.

---

[3] Arnold Hauser, *The Social History of Art* (New York: Alfred A. Knopf, Inc., 1952), p. 959.

A knowledge of art principles is also valuable in the selection and purchase of personal items, such as jewelry or automobiles. Not only may objects of pleasing design thus be secured, but they are likely to be better investments as well.

Direct personal involvement in aesthetically oriented creative activity is now recognized as widely desirable at all age levels. Some art educators believe that the individual who participates in creative art activities may derive certain of the following values:

1. Increased willingness and ability to express himself uniquely;
2. Recognition of the importance and validity of individual expression in his own as well as in others' work;
3. Improved emotional stability and mental alertness;
4. Improved concentration, interest span, patience, work habits, and use of leisure time;
5. Ability to see, understand, and appreciate aesthetic qualities in nature and in certain manmade and machine-produced objects.
6. Ability to see, understand, and appreciate aesthetic values in literature, cinema, drama, poetry, music, and the dance, as well as in painting and sculpture.

Creative art expression is believed to be a natural birthright of the child. Given art materials and even minimal encouragement, he creates easily, rapidly, and often on a high aesthetic level. Through skillful art instruction, individuals can continue creative productivity at a high (though seldom professional) level of artistic quality throughout their lives. The important human values such expression affords makes it imperative that creative art experiences be made widely and regularly available, particularly during the highly influential elementary and secondary school years.

If art were permitted to play its natural and essential role in human life, it would probably have pronounced effects upon improved individual welfare and upon nearly every element of the environment in which people live, work, study, and play. One can only speculate about the nature of a society in which art reached all people, since never in history have more than a minority enjoyed its many benefits. With the vast improvements in economic conditions, mass communications, and education found in many parts of the world today, we are provided as never before with many of the conditions necessary for a widespread and effective infusion of the arts into human life.

Throughout history, individuals—and, later, organizations—have shared their interest in and knowledge (even ownership) of works of art with the public. By donating works of art and money to museums, by converting private homes containing art collections into public institutions, by sponsoring lectures and publications, and by endowing art programs and art schools, philanthropic individuals and groups have made works of art and information concerning them available to millions of people.

But if art is to be understood and if its values are to be effective, art must be experienced more frequently and over longer periods of time than is usually possible through rare visits to museums. Millions of people throughout the world have practically no contact with works of art and receive no formal art education. For those who see art as a desirable and necessary means of improving human life, nothing less than major governmental contributions to the support of the arts can be considered adequate. Not even a doubling of the present number of art museums, educational programs, and mass communication media would bring the arts within reach of the millions of persons whose lives are now almost completely unaffected by these superb products of human aesthetic endeavor. To those who are critical of governmental support of the arts, one can only point to the urgency of the present need for aesthetic values in human life and cite the widely acclaimed success of government-sponsored art programs in the State of New York and in many countries throughout the world. To argue about the potential danger of governmental control of the arts in the face of such evidence and in light of the public need is needlessly to condemn millions of unenlightened persons to artistic ignorance. As Senator Hubert H. Humphrey has said:

> It is essential to the general welfare and to the national interest to encourage creative activity in the performance and practice of the arts, and a widespread participation in and appreciation of the arts.[4]

Summary

The historic evidence and contemporary theories presented in this chapter should convince anyone who is doubtful that the arts are

---

[4] Hubert H. Humphrey, "The Cultural Arts and the Nation," *Arts in Society* (Fall, 1960), 11.

absolutely essential to contemporary human life, and that they must be brought, not merely be made available, to all persons. Clearly, the most effective means of bringing art to the public is through education.

CHAPTER III

The Role of Art in Education

Historical Development

Art education, as we know it today, was nonexistent before the nineteenth century. Whatever art knowledge individuals might have gained was acquired indirectly through the occasional viewing of engraved reproductions, through the even rarer contacts with original paintings and sculpture, through the apprentice training of persons who had demonstrated artistic talent and found sympathetic masters, and, of course, through the environment which was on a generally higher aesthetic plane than the billboard-cluttered, architecturally styleless setting in which we find ourselves today.

Art education as a formal element of American schooling was introduced in the early nineteenth century as an adjunct to the social education of young women. Needlepoint, oil painting on glass and velvet, and pencil drawing were introduced. Resultant works were of little artistic value, yet they were regarded—by those who made them and by their families—as original art works of high quality.

During the nineteenth century, art education was gradually added to the curricula of various institutions and was eventually extended to coeducational and boys' schools and to the emerging educational programs of art museums. Nevertheless it remained primarily inartistic in nature. Art appreciation was added to instructional programs, but it, too, was basically inartistic because it dealt superficially with the subject matter of works of art rather than with their aesthetic qualities. America's failure to produce a significant number of great artists and the fundamental aesthetic illiteracy of the nation during the nineteenth and early twentieth centuries must have been largely owing to the inadequacy of programs of art education in schools and museums.

Not until the second and third decades of the twentieth century did art educators begin to offer the kind of instruction which is now

32

known to provide a foundation for sound aesthetic judgment and significant artistic productivity. The gradual abandonment of unsatisfactory methods of teaching art was brought about as a result of the implementation of theories developed early in the twentieth century by Franz Cizek in Vienna, by the faculty of the Bauhaus in Weimar and Dessau, and by other pioneering individuals and groups. A number of American art educators can be credited with having refined and validated these theories. Walter Gropius, who gave many years of valuable leadership to American art education, speaks of the urgency of an excellent art education:

> . . . our society [should] see to it that our educational system for the next generation will develop in each child, from the beginning, a perceptive awareness which intensifies his sense of form. . . . Our present methods of education which put a premium on accumulation of knowledge, have rarely reached out to include a training in creative habits of observing, seeing and shaping our surroundings. . . . Children should be introduced right from the start to the potentialities of their environment, to the physical and psychological laws that govern the visual world and to the supreme enjoyment that comes from participating in the creative process of giving form to one's living space. Such experience, if continued in depth throughout the whole of the educational cycle, will never be forgotten and will prepare the adult to continue taking an informed interest in what happens around him.[1]

Contemporary Art Education

A rapidly increasing number of enlightened art teachers are offering the children—and often the adults—of their communities instructional programs in the arts which, at their best, simultaneously develop creative ability in art expression and an understanding of the world's art heritage. Art teachers have all but abandoned stereotyped methods of teaching art expression and most of them have stopped offering meaningless "art appreciation" lessons. Striking progress has been noted in the art educational programs of the United States, the Scandinavian countries, England, Canada, Japan, and several other countries. The result of this general transformation

---

[1] Walter Gropius, in an address given upon his receipt of an honorary degree of Doctor of Humane Letters from Columbia University, March 21, 1961. Reported in *Arts and Architecture* (May, 1961), 28, 29.

of art education should soon show significant results in terms of vastly increased artistic creativity and in greater understanding of the arts. Although no system of art education has ever been (or is likely to be) able actually to produce artists, greatly improved and vastly extended programs of art education should make it possible for more latent artistic talent to be discovered and brought to fruition and should help to develop an art-educated public which will form a cultural milieu in which the arts can flourish. Never before in world history has such a broad segment of the population been as well informed about, as fully exposed to, and as productive in, the arts. If, through fortunate circumstance, a sizable number of artists were to grow more or less simultaneously in this culturally rich soil as they did during the Renaissance, humanity should once again be richly and lastingly benefited.

Like members of other vigorous, growing professions, art educators have their points of philosophic agreement and disagreement. We shall first consider prevailing, though sometimes contrasting, art educational theories and practices, and then set forth a balanced philosophy of art education which attempts to include the best features of each.

Prevailing Learning Theories and Teaching Practices in American Art Education

Although many American (and a number of foreign) art educators would probably endorse most of the learning theories and teaching practices in art education which are described below, the way in which they would interpret and implement them would unquestionably vary. This type of variance is, however, characteristic of many professions. A professional person is entitled, within ethical limitations, to bring to the generally accepted body of beliefs in his field his own interpretations of, and contributions to, theory and practice. Until a theory has been proven false or is widely disclaimed by professional leaders, art educators are justified in adhering to it.

Directed teaching is a term often used by art educators to define a kind of teaching in which stereotyped, step-by-step, copying, tracing, or imitative procedures are utilized. It is probably the only prevailing practice which has been shown to be harmful in part and outmoded as a whole by most major professional organizations and leaders in art education. Yet even among art educators who sub-scribe to the theory of creative teaching there are some who occa-sionally utilize directed teaching methods.

Furthermore, many classroom teachers and parents provide out-lined illustrations for children to fill in (a procedure which has been shown to be harmful to the development of children's conceptual and expressive abilities) [2] or permit the use of coloring books, num-bered painting sets, and precut craft kits (which are similar enough to fill-in illustrations to be considered harmful). Some art teachers and classroom teachers make illustrations or models or pass out reproductions of artists' works for pupils to copy (a procedure widely frowned upon, but not proven harmful). A larger number of teachers made "corrections" on, or additions to, students' art work (a procedure frowned upon by some, but not proven harmful). An even larger number of art teachers provide reference material in the form of photographs of various subjects or reproductions of works of art for students to study and interpret, but not copy (a pro-cedure frowned upon by some art educators, although there is no pub-lished evidence to prove it harmful). The divergence of opinion between the seemingly valid but still unsubstantiated beliefs of a dozen or more art educational theorists on the one hand and many thousands of presumably intelligent and well-meaning art teachers on the other makes it clear that much further thought and research must be devoted to the subject of creativity and imitation. Probably no art teacher would disclaim the many values inherent in aesthetically ori-ented creative art expression (see pp. 29, 40, 41). This seems to be the form of art teaching that is most frequently practiced. Yet there are many art teachers who are unwilling to dismiss so obvious and im-portant a factor of human psychology as the desire and occasional need to imitate. Such teachers know that children learn to speak, to read, to write, and to do many other things by imitating others, and that such practices apparently have not harmed subsequent creative expression in these fields. They also know that many distinguished artists throughout history have imitated their favorite masters.

It is likely that future art educational theory will suggest means by which the quality of outstanding art works might be more effec-tively studied and emulated without being copied. Until such time

---

[2] Irene Russell and Blanche Waugaman, "A Study of the Effect of Workbook Copy Experiences on the Creative Concepts of Children," Eastern Arts Association *Research Bulletin*, Vol. 3, No. 1 (April, 1952), 8–9.

as a theory of artistic creativity and imitation is more fully developed and better substantiated, it is likely that a sizable number of art teachers will continue to let their best judgment be their guide.

Laissez-faire teaching is a term used to describe a situation in which pupils are permitted to do pretty much what they please, when they wish, and in any way they choose, as long as they work "creatively" and behave themselves. Laissez-faire art education ranges from complete irresponsibility to competent, creative teaching. It came about largely as a mild but misguided revolt against the forms of directed teaching which were dominant in the early twentieth century. Some art teachers whose methods may best be described as laissez-faire wrongly imagine that these are in harmony with the philosophy of John Dewey and the progressive educational movement.

Child-centered teaching refers to a situation in which the child's happiness and welfare and the growth of his total personality is regarded as all-important, and in which special subjects (such as art) are introduced only as called for by the "total needs" of the moment. Some advocates of this method believe the elementary school teacher is the person best suited for teaching all subjects to her pupils because she knows their personalities, their needs, and their strengths and weaknesses better than special teachers of art and other subjects might. Supporters of the child-centered teaching theory should, of course, be helped to realize that art teachers are usually as much concerned with individual children and their needs as anyone else, and that they, too, have been trained in child psychology and the general theories of elementary education. It is difficult to imagine that there could be more than a few gifted classroom teachers who possess enough training in language arts, social sciences, art, music, the dance, biological and physical sciences, and mathematics to be able to teach these subjects as well as a team of elementary school subject specialists who attempt to supplement and enrich regular classroom experiences. To train significant numbers of classroom teachers for the assumption of total responsibility for their pupils' educational needs, if this could indeed be done, would require at least twice the number of years now needed for elementary school teacher preparation.

A number of art educators indirectly support the child-centered theory of education through their teaching methods. They feel that picture-making, through which children reveal their inner interests and needs by illustrating themselves and their family, friends, and environment, is the most desirable form of art education. Child-centered art educators minimize and sometimes even frown upon such art activities as three-dimensional construction, collage-making, and abstract painting. Although they are correct in their belief that the making of representational pictures provides important clues to the child's personality, needs, and interests, they are wrong in believing that nonillustrative art activity is mere play and that abstract paintings and constructions might not even more clearly reveal certain vital aspects of personality structure.

Art educators who support the child-centered theory of education are often devotees of psychologically oriented art educational research in which certain types of personality are believed to be revealed through creative expression. Some go so far as to adopt rather specific (and often limiting) psychological classifications devised by art educational theorists and tailor their teaching to what are believed to be the special needs of persons in a particular category. Such practices are, however, generally frowned upon by psychologists as well as by many art educators who consider them to be founded upon inconclusive research.

A sizable number of contemporary art educators emphasize experimentation with materials. It is their belief (and to a point they are correct) that the use of materials—wood, paint, clay, feathers, and bits of cloth—is in itself highly educative. They believe that by experimenting with a wide variety of materials, pupils learn important qualities such as the discipline inherent in the manipulative limitations of wood, the varying fluidity of different kinds of paints, and the effect of light upon color and texture. Perhaps most important to proponents of such experimenting is the belief that it facilitates and increases the flow of creative expression, and that uninhibited, materials-oriented self-expression builds confidence and develops skills.

At their worst, art educators who stress experimentation with materials are practicing a laissez-faire philosophy embellished with bright colors and rich textures. At their best, art educators who use many materials in their teaching have carefully studied the philosophy, methodology, and products of the early twentieth century Bauhaus, where this approach to art education was conceived, and have

maintained its original high level of quality. Such art teachers carefully balance experimentation with instruction and simultaneously
encourage freedom and craftsmanship, spontaniety and thoughtful
expression, and representation as well as interpretation and pure design. They distinguish themselves from other enlightened art educators mainly by their provision of wider varieties of materials,
especially those of a three-dimensional nature. A tremendous effort
is required to identify, collect, organize, store, distribute, provide
instruction for, and arrange the cleanup of the hundreds of materials
which such a program might utilize. Persons who skillfully practice
this theory of art education have exerted widespread and important
influences upon those of their colleagues who have limited their programs of art education to traditional and often restrictive media such
as pencils, crayons, watercolors, and poster paint.

One of the newer philosophic emphases in contemporary art education might be termed *cultural context*. Long overdue in education,
it sees art study and expression in the broad setting of such related
academic disciplines as history, sociology, philosophy, and psychology. Art educators who subscribe to this philosophy attempt to
provide their pupils, even in the elementary school grades, with the
highest possible level of liberal arts education. They work cooperatively with classroom teachers, with specialists in fields such as music
and drama, and with parents and professionals in the community to
offer skillfully integrated subject study at every grade level. The
successful implementation of this type of art education obviously
requires teachers who have strong backgrounds in the liberal arts.
It calls for art teachers who wish to enrich and intensify their pupils'
learning experiences by supplementing art expression and study with
special reading assignments, lectures, discussions, films and slides,
field trips, demonstrations, and visits by professional artists. At its
finest, this form of art education is markedly superior to earlier,
comparatively feeble efforts to integrate school subjects which used
art merely to illustrate various topics of current interest. At its best,
cultural context art education retains the aesthetic identity of the
arts, fosters significant art expression, and contributes richly to
pupils' learning experiences in other subjects.

One of the most recent, and perhaps most promising, emphases in
art educational philosophy has been termed *aesthetically oriented
creative art teaching*. It developed as a result of dissatisfaction with

earlier practices in which the study of art and the attainment of significant aesthetic quality in art expression were neglected. Proponents of aesthetically oriented creative art teaching want their pupils to develop an understanding of the arts of all periods and to strive for the attainment of the highest possible level of quality in their own creative works. One proponent of this philosophic view in art education says:

> . . . the theoretical justification for education in serious art lies in the claim that it trains the feeling side of life just as other studies train the intellectual side and still others perfect bodily skills, and that it does so in a way that goes beyond the educative effects of popular art.[3]

Art educators who implement this philosophy make extensive use of original art works as well as slides, reproductions, films, field trips, and guest lecturers to introduce their pupils to masterpieces of painting, sculpture, architecture, and various forms of applied art. They make fairly extensive use of these examples as instructional aids and as standards against which they measure the creative art activities of their pupils. They display important art works (or reproductions) in the art room in which pupils create and study, in other classrooms, and in corridors in order that these works may become gradually understood in a familiar setting.

Advocates of aesthetically oriented creative art education believe in active teaching. They lecture, answer questions as specifically as possible, and give detailed criticisms of pupils' art works. They use texts, reference books, magazines, mimeographed material, charts, and diagrams. They give specific and frequent reading assignments and ask for written reports. They also require homework in the form of sketches and other types of creative work. Those who teach in schools in or near cities with art galleries or museums conduct field trips and require students to make periodic visits to such institutions during out-of-school hours. Practitioners of aesthetically oriented creative art teaching make special efforts to maintain an up-to-date knowledge of the arts, education, and the liberal arts. They regularly engage in personal creative activity and, if possible, exhibit their work. Increasingly, they contribute to the literature of their profession and play active roles in professional organizations. They

---

[3] H. S. Broudy, "The Case for Art Education," *Athene* (Winter, 1961), 7.

work diligently and aggressively to provide the kind of art education they believe to be best.

A Balanced Philosophy
of Art Education

Each of these theories of art education contains elements worthy of continued implementation. But all of them need further study and research; some need to be reinterpreted, revised, or brought up to date. Certain aspects need far wider application before their worth can be fairly judged.

Art educators are developing a balanced philosophy of art education which contains the most desirable elements of past and present theories and practices. More often than not, their philosophy is tailored to fit their own beliefs, the needs and interests of their pupils, and the nature of the local environment. There is a clear and probably desirable trend away from identification with particular philosophic camps or individual spokesmen. Art educators have gained considerable maturity in recent years. They are better and more fully trained than their predecessors and the higher quality of their education has made them unwilling to accept philosophic tenets in which they do not believe, no matter how widely these may be practiced or how loudly they may be heralded. Even as undergraduate students, art-teachers-to-be often respectfully disagree with ideas presented by their professors or by their textbooks, and are given opportunity to explain and, if possible, to document their views.

The following elements of a balanced philosophy of art education are offered as generally characteristic of the professional theories and practices which are currently regarded as desirable. They have been validated in whole or in part through research, or they have been practiced long enough and widely enough to prove their worth. Most of these elements have emanated from the writings or teachings of such distinguished art educators, artists, art historians, and philosophers as Cizek, D'Amico, Dewey, Gropius, Hauser, Langer, Logan, Lowenfeld, Malraux, Mumford, Munro, Read, and Taylor (see Bibliography).

1. Art is a fundamental element of human life; it is a major discipline as essential to education as the language arts and the sciences.

Both the ability to express oneself creatively in a variety of media and a knowledge of major art forms of the past and present are of the highest importance to all human beings. Art education contributes significantly to essential human needs by developing the ability to respond creatively to various stimuli; by making constructive use of the tendency to rank and imitate things; by encouraging the expression of profound beliefs and the revelation of subconscious attitudes; by heightening perception of essences and details as well as of relationships; by encouraging the creation and/or enjoyment of objects of great artistic significance; by developing the ability to make personally and socially constructive as well as more pleasing use of leisure time; by providing a balance for the stress on scientific, political, and military matters; by providing an antidote to conformist and materialist pressures found in large organizations, the mass communication media, certain forms of suburban living, and even in children's toys and games; by contributing to intellectual growth; by enhancing the ability to organize disparate elements; by improving emotional sensitivity and balance; and by strengthening the total personality.

In addition, it is believed that art education provides an internationally communicable visual language, makes possible a visual documentation of contemporary culture, and aids in the visual interpretation of societies of the past.

2. All persons should receive a thorough education in art, beginning in nursery school or kindergarten and continuing throughout secondary school, college, and adult life.

3. An education in art should include a wide variety of opportunities for personal creative expression; an intensive study of the works of major painters, sculptors, architects, craftsmen, and designers; and related studies of important works in literature, music, and other academic fields.

4. All persons are capable of developing proficiency in one or more forms of creative art expression and they can be helped to develop an understanding of the arts; but such ability and knowledge cannot be acquired in capsule form, by means of do-it-yourself kits or short courses on art appreciation, or from poorly qualified teachers.

5. Major and lasting contributions to individual welfare, community and national life, and international relations can be made

through a widespread and intensive study of and participation in the arts. For this reason, governmental aid to and support of the arts is imperative.

6. At all educational levels, including the primary grades, art should be taught by a specialist who has had four or more years of preparation, who understands the complex delicacy of the creative process in art and is able to nourish its growth, who is well-prepared in art history, and who can foster the development of aesthetic value judgments on all types of fine and applied art objects.

It is further believed that supplemental art educational experiences should be provided by classroom teachers, teachers of other special subjects, parents, and the environments in which we live.

7. Personal art expression is best fostered through aesthetically oriented creative art teaching and, conversely, personal art expression is hampered by teaching methods which exclude aesthetic considerations and rely upon copying or other stereotyped procedures.

8. A knowledge of art is best fostered through broad studies of periods and styles; through depth studies of major works within particular periods and styles; through emphasis upon the aesthetic qualities which underlie and interrelate the arts, rather than memorization of names, dates, and places; through personal creative work in media related to the periods and styles being studied; and through carefully planned correlation of art studies with other subjects.

9. A modest collection of original art works, frequent field trips, an extensive collection of color slides and reproductions, art films, and a complete stock of art supplies are essential to the implementation of a program of art education.

Summary

In its comparatively brief history, art education has grown from a state of superficial dilletantism to a level of essential human significance. A variety of art learning theories and teaching practices are merging into a balanced philosophy by which future generations may be served more effectively.

CHAPTER IV

The Teaching of Art

One of the most active professional debates in the history of art education has taken place during the past decade. It has centered about the question of who is best qualified to teach art to children. Until very recently, in fact, professional opinion was divided: some believed that specially prepared art teachers were best qualified for this role; others felt that elementary classroom teachers were better suited for teaching art as well as all other subjects. The difference in professional opinion arose because of a misunderstanding of the art consultant concept which had been advocated by a number of art educators, educational theorists, and school administrators. The more enlightened advocates of art consultation wanted to extend and intensify the teaching of art both by art teachers and by classroom teachers. Unfortunately, in their implementation of the art consultant concept, a number of school administrators and art educational supervisors all but eliminated the actual teaching of art by specialists: they converted art teachers into on-call advisors whose main responsibility was to help classroom teachers. But in its original form, the art consultant concept called for more rather than less art teaching; hence the heated professional debate on this topic has been unnecessary. It was useful, however, in clarifying and, more recently, in resolving the art teacher's essential role in elementary education.

The consensus among professionals now is:

1. Specially prepared teachers of art are needed at all grade levels in the elementary school, primarily to teach art to children and, secondarily, to work more closely with classroom teachers in providing supplemental activities and in training these teachers through in-service workshops for the assumption of increased (but not complete) and more effective responsibility for children's art education.

2. Elementary school classroom teachers should provide materials and, to the extent of their qualifications, guidance in supplementary art experiences. They should seek to increase their qualifications by means

43

of consultative help from the art teacher, graduate courses, in-service workshops, professional conferences, and independent reading.

3. Elementary schools which do not presently employ art teachers should take steps to add them to the faculty on the basis of one art teacher for every three hundred pupils (actually, a 1:150–180 ratio can be justified: see suggested art teaching schedule on pp. 46–47). Until such time as a special art teacher is available, the classroom teacher best qualified for this role should, if she is willing, be given time to offer as much as possible of the special art instruction that pupils need. In addition, other classroom teachers should spend more than the usual amount of time (at least half a day each week) in guiding children's creative and appreciative experiences in the visual arts.

There has been less confusion on the junior and senior high school and college levels, where it has long been clearly understood that special teachers are required for competent instruction in art, music, literature, the dance, homemaking, industrial arts, mathematics, and science.

Persons Who Teach Art

Though art teachers are the persons primarily responsible for the teaching of art, many others also teach art, though often indirectly, occasionally unsatisfactorily, and sometimes harmfully. Art education is also provided by the environment in which people live, work, attend school, play, and worship. In order to overcome the frequently negative influences exerted by unqualified people and aesthetically poor environments, art teachers need to possess great skill, forthrightness, and energy.

Art teachers.   Specially prepared teachers of art are the persons best qualified for teaching art in elementary and secondary schools, colleges, universities, professional art schools, and adult education programs. But because of a shortage of qualified teachers, an increase in school population, and other problems, probably only a third of the pupils in American elementary and secondary schools receive even infrequent instruction from a teacher of art. The need for art education specialists at all educational levels is now widely acknowledged. Elementary and secondary schools throughout the country are actively seeking art teachers, and their administrators are pressuring colleges of education and art schools to increase art education enrollments in order to meet the growing professional demand.

Most American elementary and secondary school art teachers are prepared by teachers colleges, university colleges, or schools of education. A smaller but increasing number are prepared by professional art schools and institutes. Others are prepared by first receiving an undergraduate liberal arts education with a major in fine arts, then taking courses in the teaching of art and related subjects as part of an additional year of graduate study at a college or school of education.

Certification requirements for art teachers vary widely from state to state. Most states require a bachelor's degree,[1] with minimum credit requirements in certain areas specified as follows: [2]

	Semester Credits
Courses in painting, sculpture, graphic art, design, and the history of art	6–58
Art education courses (including student teaching)	2–15
Professional education courses	4–27
Liberal arts courses	6–60

Some states, such as New York, specify the exact number of credits required in each of these (and other) areas while other states automatically certify graduates of those art teacher education departments whose curricula have been approved. The national trend in art teacher certification is toward increasingly higher requirements in each of the above-mentioned categories (or, in the case of states with extremely low or unusually high requirements in certain areas, toward a more sensible distribution of point requirements).

Elementary school art teachers.   Sometimes known as art consultants, art resource persons, and art helping teachers, elementary school art teachers usually offer direct and periodic instruction to Grades 1–6 and, sometimes, Grades 1–8. In addition, many of them are available for supplemental work with classroom teachers. Under ideal circumstances they offer two hours of specialized instruction per week to each class; offer advanced instruction to children with

---

[1] Some states now require a master's degree, particularly for secondary school teaching certificates.

[2] Based on statistics presented in "A Study of Certification Requirements for Teachers of Art in the United States," Ralph G. Beelke *Research in Art Education,* Yearbook of the National Art Education Association (Kutztown, Pa.: The Association, 1954), pp. 28–77.

TABLE 1

SUGGESTED ART TEACHING SCHEDULE
FOR A 300-360 PUPIL ELEMENTARY SCHOOL *

PRIMARY GRADES ART TEACHER

	Monday	Tuesday	Wednesday	Thursday	Friday	Saturday
8:45–9			PREPARATION			"Open Studio" for recreational art groups, 10:00 A.M.–3:00 P.M.
9 –10	1A	3A	1A	3A	2A	
10 –11		STACK AND UNLOAD KILN		STACK AND UNLOAD KILN		
				PREPARATION FOR CLASSES		
11 –12	Consultation	3B	2A	3B	1B	
12 –1	Lunch	Lunch	Lunch	Lunch	Lunch	
1 –1:30		PREPARATION FOR CLASSES		Consultation	Art Club	
1:30–2:30	2B	1B	2B			
2:30–3	Cleanup	Cleanup .... Issue Supplies	Cleanup	Issue Supplies	Early Dismissal	

INTERMEDIATE GRADES ART TEACHER

	Monday	Tuesday	Wednesday	Thursday	Friday	Saturday
8:45–9	PREPARATION					"Open Studio" for recreational art groups, 10:00 A.M.–3:00 P.M.
9 –10	4A	6A	4A	6A	5A	
10 –11	STACK AND UNLOAD KILN			STACK AND UNLOAD KILN	.... PREPARATION FOR CLASSES	
11 –12	Consultation	6B	5A	6B	4B	
12 –1	Lunch	Lunch	Lunch	Lunch	Lunch	
1 –1:30	PREPARATION FOR CLASSES					
1:30–2:30	5B	4B	5B	Consultation	Art Club	
2:30–3	Cleanup	Cleanup .... Issue Supplies	Cleanup	Issue Supplies	Early Dismissal	

* Based on ideal ratio of one teacher to 150–180 pupils, and calling for two art teachers and two fully equipped art rooms. The Saturday "Open Studio" would be under the supervision of trained art specialists. "Regular" art teachers would receive extra compensation if they chose to render this service.

special interests or abilities; provide time for consultative work with classroom teachers, parents, and administrators; prepare for and evaluate classes they teach; and care for such necessary routines as ordering, arranging, and inventorying supplies and equipment. A suggestion as to how these responsibilities might be scheduled is shown in Table 1.

Frequently, elementary school art teachers correlate lessons with current classroom studies, not only to enrich these learning experiences for pupils (and their teachers) but also to take advantage of rich stimuli and various reference materials which have been secured by classroom teachers.

The elementary school art teacher's primary role, however, is not the embellishment of other subjects through illustration or model-making, but the teaching of art. Basically, this responsibility can be divided into two main areas, both requiring years of specialized professional preparation, and both ruling out the possibility of having classroom teachers assume full responsibility for the art education of their pupils.

One of the elementary school art teacher's main responsibilities is the development of children's creative expression through a wide variety of art media, processes, and activities. Here, the art teacher's role is distinctive and of utmost importance. Her concern is with the development of a special kind of creative expression—one which is aesthetically oriented and in which the highest possible quality of conceptual development (enrichment and refinement of ideas and feelings to be expressed), composition, color relationships, texture, and other artistic elements and principles are taught to and employed by pupils. Numerous methods of teaching children to express themselves through art in ways which are aesthetic as well as creative have been developed in recent years. Though each art teacher's approach is unique, most of them employ in one form or another the following teaching procedures:

1. Provide desirable human relationships and environmental and other conditions which enhance creative expression (see pp. 12–13).

2. Gear art activities to pupils' needs and interests.

3. Provide such appropriate stimuli as field trips, original art works, reproductions, slides, films, filmstrips, guest lecturers, readings (prior to, in, and after class) in literature and other subjects

as well as in art, pantomime, art games, spontaneous storytelling, and rhythmic body movements.

4. Give specific (though not inhibiting or stereotyped instruction and criticism; not "Do what you like in whatever way you like, with whatever media you like, whenever you like," but perhaps "Today I thought you might like to make clay models of your pet or of your favorite animal." The teacher might add, for example:

> When we look at animals we think certain things about them. Why does the elephant "feel" big and heavy? ... Do you think his track will be printed deeply into the ground? How could you show the slow, lumbering walk of an elephant swaying his trunk as he moves along? Can you show this with your body? If you made a heavy elephant in clay, how could you make his legs strong enough for him to stand? How could you make a trunk that would not break and fall off? [3]

This might be followed (or preceded) by careful observation and discussion of pets brought to school or observed on field trips; a study of photographs, slides, or films of pets and other animals; and a study of professional art works (Delacroix, Degas, Marc, and others) in which animals have been interpreted in different ways. The art teacher or experienced pupils might demonstrate some of the ways of modeling clay; explain (to individuals or small groups) how to make legs stick to bodies and how to use bits of wire or wood as armatures for tails or ears; elicit suggestions on ways of achieving various textural effects with pencil points, combs, embedded feathers, sawdust, and pebbles; make instructive comments (not always "That's nice! Keep working," but "I like the way you have turned the head to one side," or "You can bend the legs to show him walking or sitting down, if you wish); and, at least once during the activity period and again at the end, lead a group critique in which the art qualities, craftsmanship, interpretations, and techniques in each child's work are discussed and constructively evaluated.

The other main responsibility of the elementary school art teacher is the development of children's understanding of the arts through a study of original art works, slides, reproductions, films, photographs, and filmstrips. Here, again, the art teacher's role is distinctive

---

[3] Kelly Fearing, Clyde Martin, and Evelyn Beard, *Our Expanding Vision,* Book II (Austin, Texas: W. S. Benson & Co., 1960), p. 25.

and important. Drawing upon knowledge acquired in college art history courses, independent reading, visits to art galleries and museums, personal creative work, and acquaintance with other artists, the elementary school art teacher assigns readings (with oral and written reports), conducts field trips, and provides examples of historic and contemporary painting, sculpture, architecture and community planning, the graphic arts, photography, industrial design, the crafts, and advertising design. She carefully chooses aesthetically significant art works which are within the interest range of each group of pupils and, through class presentations and discussions, develops the pupils' understanding of those qualities and basic principles which are found in most forms of art expression and those which are characteristic of the work of particular artists, schools, and styles. She builds upon her pupils' inherent aesthetic sensitivity and teaches them to employ it in making critical value judgments on works they study.

At each succeeding grade level, the time spent on the study of works of art is increased until, by the sixth grade, pupils spend as much as a third of their art class time on this phase of the subject. This means that increasingly less time can be devoted to the art teacher's guidance of pupils' creative expression (unless additional time and art teaching personnel can be provided) and that elementary schools must provide funds for slides, filmstrips, reproductions, photographs, films, and at least a few original works of art.

Secondary school art teachers. Such teachers usually teach required courses to pupils in Grades 7 and/or 8, and elective courses (based on the art teacher's special competencies as well as on pupil interests) to pupils in Grades 9–12. Present teaching practices place greater stress upon guiding pupils' art expression than upon developing their knowledge of painting, sculpture, architecture, and related fields. Leading professional opinion calls for a sharp increase in the study of professional art works at this level and urges school systems to require all pupils to take four art courses, both in Grades 7 and 8 and again in Grades 9 or 10 and 11 or 12. It is believed that required general art courses for all pupils (including art majors who would take additional, elective studio courses) should devote approximately one third of the time to art expression and two thirds to the study of the arts.

Secondary school art teaching methods are similar to those employed at the elementary school level, but much greater stress is placed upon detailed and (especially for those pupils who want to major in art) constructively critical evaluation of the art qualities found, or lacking, in works produced by pupils. In the study of art works, class presentations are longer and more scholarly in nature than in the elementary grades and more extensive use is made of the school's collection of art works, slides, and reproductions, as well as of field trips, reading assignments, and gallery or museum visits.

Required art courses at the secondary school level range in length from twenty to forty weeks, and in time from two to five hours per week. Elective courses usually meet for three to five hours per week for twenty weeks. Leading professional opinion calls for each required course at the seventh- and eighth-grade levels to meet at least three hours per week for forty weeks, and for elective courses (some—such as crafts and painting—for non-art majors, and several—such as painting, sculpture, architecture, crafts, clothing design, and mechanical drawing—for art majors) to meet for five hours per week for twenty weeks.

College and professional school art instructors. Instructors at these levels are not required to meet conventional teacher certificational standards. Their preparation, interests, knowledge, expressive skills, and teaching assignments are usually more specialized. In fact, their highly successful performance in American colleges, universities, and professional art schools have caused many states to increase (but to make less general) the certification requirements for elementary and secondary school teachers of art.

Most college and professional school art instructors (especially those teaching art education and art history courses) have master's degrees, some have doctorates, and many (especially those teaching studio courses) have professional art school diplomas or degrees. But a sizable number of instructors, especially those who teach studio courses in large metropolitan areas, have no colleges degrees and may not even have an art school diploma. Most of these instructors are established professional artists whose experience, reputation, and—in many cases—demonstrated teaching ability are accepted as adequate qualifications for the positions they hold. Though most well-known artists who teach in colleges and professional art schools presently do so only on a part-time basis, increasing numbers of them are accepting full-time assignments as professors or artists-in-residence.

Full-time teaching assignments for college and professional art school instructors range from a high of twenty-five to a low of seven or eight hours of instruction per week—the smaller number of assigned hours usually being reserved for those whose services are most highly regarded by the administration. Full-time assignments in the art departments of private and liberal arts colleges and universities tend to require fewer hours of teaching than those in professional art schools and state- or city-supported colleges and universities. Artists-in-residence positions usually involve few, if any, assigned teaching hours, but incumbents are expected to admit students to their studios and to enrich the college art program in other ways.

According to their rank and full- or part-time status, college and professional school art instructors teach from one to five or six courses, each of which may meet for thirty (lecture courses) to 120 (studio courses) hours during a fifteen-week semester. The important problem of properly balancing art expression with art subject study is solved in most institutions of higher learning because students are required to take a certain number of studio courses and art history courses. College and professional school art instructors generally specialize in one of the two areas, though some teach both.

Classroom Teachers and Specialists in Subjects other than Art

Of the hundreds of thousands of teachers in American schools and colleges, only a small percentage are specially prepared teachers of art; yet teachers of all subjects at all educational levels contribute either positively or negatively to the art education of their pupils. The type of illustrative material they use, their attitude toward and knowledge of the arts of the past and the present—even the way they dress and decorate their classrooms—influence the pupils they teach.

Elementary school classroom teachers are, more often than not (but seldom by preference), teachers of art as well. In many cases they must also be teachers of music, the dance, homemaking, industrial arts, speech therapy, even foreign languages, if these special areas are included in the curriculum. Elementary school teachers of art and other special subjects are still comparatively rare, and it will be many years before the desired ratio of one art teacher for every three or four hundred elementary school pupils is realized. Until that time, elementary school classroom teachers will have to assume responsibility for the art education of their pupils. One can only hope that colleges preparing classroom teachers will increase requirements in art and other subjects in which there is a shortage of qualified specialists. As an absolute minimum, colleges should require elementary education majors to take a course in the philosophy and methods of teaching art; a studio course in painting, sculpture, and crafts; and a course in the history of art. Each course should be offered for at least three hours for fifteen weeks. Ideally, elementary education majors would take two courses in each of these three areas.

In elementary schools where art teachers are not available, classroom teachers must assume responsibility for instruction in this area. If their preparation in art education has been inadequate, they must remedy this through graduate or in-service study and independent reading (see Bibliography). Administrators should facilitate such study by arranging art workshops; by securing lecturers and temporary art consultants or supervisors; by providing time, service credit, and even tuition grants for graduate study in art education; and by training teachers through skilled supervision. But administrators and board members should take steps to hire qualified art teachers at the earliest opportunity.

Whether by choice or assignment, the classroom teacher who assumes responsibility for the art education of her pupils must make every effort to approximate the quality and scope of the program recommended for her grade level (see pp. 62–73). She must take particular care to contribute to her pupils' understanding of the arts through field trips, illustrated presentations, reading and picture-clipping assignments, discussions of reproductions and original art works hanging in the classroom and in the corridors, and especially by her genuine enthusiasm for art forms she understands and her willingness to study with her pupils those forms of art expression with which she is less familiar.

Specialists in subjects other than art, including non-art teachers of special subjects from nursery school through college and adult education programs, are as responsible for their pupils' art education as they are for their use of good English. At the very least, special teachers of subjects other than art should, by example, indicate the kind of respectful and knowledgeable attitude toward the arts which one expects mature, educated persons to show for all major fields of human endeavor. The field of art is much more than an array of paintings and other works upon which the non-art teacher is expected to express amateur value judgments. What would science educators, for example, think of an art teacher who said "Nuclear physics is meaningless. Scientists who practice it are trying to fool the public"?

Many laymen believe that what they see, feel, or understand when they look at a work of art is an adequate basis for judging it good or bad, yet the same people would not think of evaluating Einstein's $E = MC^2$ equation on so superficial a basis. Apparently, the appearance of completeness, clarity, and tangibility presented by many works of art leads casual observers to believe that what they see is all there is in a work of art. Little do they realize that mere identification of such pictorial elements as trees, clouds, and water is no more meaningful in understanding the art quality of a painting than would be the mere sequential recitation of E, M, C. The meaning of each element—and, even more important, the meaning of each element's relationship to the others—is what really matters in Einstein's famous equation.

Teachers, like other professionals, are looked upon as highly educated, mature, dependable, and authoritative persons. Even their casual remarks profoundly affect the educational development of their pupils and influence other people with whom they associate. They must practice the same openmindedness, respect, and scholarly restraint in commenting upon art as in expressing their views on other subjects. Hopefully, they will have acquired enough knowledge of the arts in college courses or through independent study to contribute to rather than impede the art educational development of their pupils.

Teachers of all subjects should be required to take at least one full-year course in the history of art as part of their undergraduate education. Such a course should include a study of historic and contemporary painting, sculpture, architecture, community planning, the graphic arts, photography, and applied design. Students should be occasionally confronted with original art works which they can study firsthand in some depth. The bulk of the course material, however, would probably be presented by means of slide-illustrated lecture-discussions.

Designers, authors, and art contributors to mass communication media. One can hardly overestimate the extent of the influences exerted by the tens of thousands of persons who design advertisements, packages, furniture, toys, and other articles; those who write or illustrate books and articles on art subjects; and those who write, design or perform for radio, television, movies, and the theater. The art judgment of millions of people is affected by the products and performances of people in these fields. Although the general level of art quality in these fields has risen rapidly in recent years, the contribution of most mass media to art education is still predominantly negative. For every outstanding designer, author, and mass media contributor in the field of art, there are hundreds whose work is of poor quality. Many of the latter, in fact, acknowledge the poor quality of their work, attempt to excuse it on the basis of "popular demand," and claim they would work at a higher level of quality if it would bring them an equal or higher income. This philosophy is obviously fallacious, cowardly, and fundamentally unethical. How sharply it contrasts with the practices of art and classroom teachers who strive to bring their pupils to the highest possible level of quality in creative expression and art knowledge! Were a majority of designers, authors, and mass media contributors in the arts willing, able, and determined to produce work of the very highest aesthetic quality, America's cultural status would quickly be raised. Art teachers would then no longer have to disappoint idealistic pupils by telling them that although persons in the mass media are capable of excellent work, most of them have purposely chosen to work at a lower level of quality. But in light of the overwhelmingly materialistic and conformist orientation of most artists, writers, and performers working in the mass media, who would dare estimate the number of years—or decades—necessary to bring about such a transformation?

Parents, other relatives, and peers. Psychologists, educators, and other enlightened adults are becoming increasingly aware of the deep and lasting effects which a child's (even an adult's) parents, relatives, and peers have upon his personality, behavior, intelligence, and sensitivity to aesthetic values. Regrettably, most of these effects are negative, even at the higher economic levels of society. Art educators are particularly concerned about the effects of coloring books and other stereotyped materials which parents and other relatives purchase for children, about the contradictions made—often unknowingly—by parents who comment upon the creative art work children bring home from school, and about the influence of poorly designed home and community environments. The natural love which all persons have for their parents and other relatives and the exceedingly great desire for peer approval cause the opinions and actions of relatives and peers to have a pronounced, often dominant, influence upon individual attitudes and behavior patterns. The broader aims of art education cannot be adequately realized until a large segment of the population has acquired a fundamental knowledge of art and of the importance of personal creative expression.

Summary

Because the teaching of art requires special skills and knowledge, the person best qualified to teach art in the schools is the one who has received preparation for work in this specific field. Because the present need for such specially prepared persons far exceeds the supply, both the elementary classroom teacher and the secondary school teacher who has specialized in other fields will be called upon to supplement the art learnings of their students. Parents, relatives, and persons who work in the mass media of communication also have a responsibility toward guiding the art education of children. If such persons are to exert the positive influence necessary to the further development of children, they must themselves acquire a broader knowledge of art and of the significance of personal creative expression.

CHAPTER V

Interest and Ability Levels in Art Education

There are no specific groups of art media, activities, and learning experiences which are unique to a particular grade or age level. The classroom teacher, art teacher, or parent who seeks categorized information in this field knows little about the fluidity of children's interest and ability levels in creative expression or about the development of art concepts. No two individuals are identical in their art expressive or conceptual abilities, nor does the fact that what they do or know in art is similar to what appear to be behavioral norms of younger or older children necessarily mean that they are artistically retarded or gifted. Giftedness in art expression (see pp. 77–78), for example, does not appear to be identifiable until adolescence or later, and art ability—or the lack of it—in childhood does not seem to be a major determining factor.

Though, as Frances Wilson has said:

> A medium that is good in one situation may not be at all suitable in another. The total situation in which a medium is used is made up of many factors such as (1) the person using it, his experience, immediate mood . . . and what he wants to express, (2) the art teacher, his personality and skill and the degree to which he can identify with and contribute to the creativity of the person using the medium, (3) the total group and the degree to which they are contributing or opposing him and the degree to which they are making demands on the teacher at the moment the person needs help, (4) and the physical setting, what it contributes to or detracts from the person using the medium.[4]

There are, nevertheless, certain art interests, abilities, media, activities, processes, and learning experiences which can be generally identified within various grade groupings or age ranges. Once he has this fundamental knowledge, the art educator attempts to develop the knowledge and skill necessary to help each child, ado-

---

[4] Frances Wilson, "Art Experience or Experience in Being" (Ithaca, N.Y.: Cornell University College of Home Economics, 1955), p. 43. Mimeographed.

lescent, or adult develop the highest degree of uniqueness and quality in his art expression and the greatest profundity in his aesthetic judgment.

The information which follows is presented in school grade-level groupings to indicate the developmental phases of art education through which all persons (at widely varying rates, and not necessarily in the order presented) pass. But the various topics within each school grade grouping, such as "Recommended Stimuli," and "Suggested Activities," are, with minor modifications, appropriate for other levels as well.

Art Education in the Home and Nursery School

Creative art expression and, later, the ability to understand the aesthetic bases of the arts, appear to be as natural to the young child as eating, sleeping, and walking. In his creative work, the young child freely, effectively, and happily expresses his thoughts and attitudes: he plays constructively, and he begins to learn the meaning of great works of art of the past and present. Most children are ready to paint and model by the time they are twelve to fifteen months old, and they are ready for introductory learning experiences through the observation of professional art works by the time they are three years old. But, unfortunately, most young children are denied both opportunities for one or more of the following reasons:

1. Only a small percentage of them attend nursery schools where creative expression is usually fostered by well-trained teachers;

2. Many parents are unwilling to expend the effort in the securing of materials, preparation, and cleanup which most creative art activities necessitate;

3. Some of the few parents who do provide clay, paint, and other art materials for their children offer the wrong kind of guidance or fail to provide other conditions which are conducive to creative art expression (see pp. 12–14);

4. Many parents and relatives provide young children with coloring books and other stereotyped materials which impede creative expression;

5. Very few homes or nursery schools contain original art works—or even reproductions—of high aesthetic quality which might even indirectly contribute to young childrens' art knowledge.

At home and/or in nursery school, the young child should readily be able to paint, model, construct, or draw, and he should receive creative guidance at appropriate times. There should be a table of proper height where he can work at times of his choice, with materials such as clay, tempera and finger paint, crayons, and paper ready for use. There should be a parent (or teacher) nearby who will give him creative guidance as needed and help him with unmanageable materials. The young child should not be shown or told how to draw, copy, or trace houses, persons, animals, and various objects. He should be effectively encouraged to think and talk about the appearance and other qualities of these things, to look at and discuss actual objects or pictures of them, and thus to enrich the concepts from which art expression emanates. He can be taught to recognize, choose, mix, paint over, and apply various colors. He can be introduced to new art materials. He can be shown how to press clay pieces together so they will stick. He can be shown how to achieve strokes of various widths with a crayon or brush. He can profit greatly by appropriate stimuli, and he can gain confidence and increased ease of expression through proper comments on the works he produces and the ways in which he produces them.

The child of two or three may merely play with paints or modeling materials, making scribbles, swirls, or informal squeezed shapes which appear meaningless. Yet to the child these experiences are important; they are believed to be expressions of his innermost feelings. Play is as serious to the young child as work is to the adult; he often applies himself to it with total interest and great effort. The adult might (if he is not told) ask "Would you like to tell me about what you are doing?" but he should probably not ask "What is that supposed to be?" or "Why did you use so much red?" The young child is deeply stimulated by many elements of his environment. He needs and wants to express his reactions to these stimuli, but the guidance he seeks and receives should be subtle, skillful, well-timed, and conducive to creative expression.

Under ideal conditions, the child should neither be pressed for time nor expected to continue working beyond the limits of his interest span. He should be able to work as long as he wishes, to make as many pictures or models as he wants, and to resume or discontinue working whenever he likes.

Among the stimuli which parents and nursery school teachers can provide are "looking walks"; trips to farms, zoos, and other places of interest; films and slides; poetry and story readings; group discussions of rainy, windy, snowy, or sunny days; careful observation and discussion of pets; guessing what is in a box which rattles; and art materials (such as finger paints or modeling dough) which the children have not previously used.

A number of media and activities are well-suited for encouraging the creative art expression of young children: among them are dough, paper pulp, and moist clay (plasticene is less satisfactory); tempera paint with long-bristle brushes of varying widths (powder paint is less intense and less opaque, and requires more preparation) and large sheets of heavy paper (say twelve by fifteen inches); large unwrapped sticks of chalk or crayon (the latter are less desirable because sustained pressure is required to attain large areas of intense color, and some children dislike the "dusty" feel and messiness of chalk and the "stickiness" of crayons); and chalk drawing and water painting on blackboards. Also recommended are vegetable and stick printing (flat-cut carrot, potato, stick, or block surfaces are covered with paint or pressed on blotters soaked in a saucer of tempera paint, then pressed on paper or cloth); wood and cardboard building blocks (which can be used to create three-dimensional designs, augmented by larger, resealed cardboard boxes); finger paint (commercial brands are comparatively inexpensive in pint size or larger jars, and are superior to most homemade types) on water proof table surfaces or large butcher trays which are often used for "warmup" painting before glazed finger paint or shelf paper is provided; and a wide variety of collage materials and adhesives, such as colored paper, round-tipped scissors, feathers, bits of cellophane and cardboard, sandpaper, cloth, soda straws, paste, glue, cellophane tape, and a stapler.

The nature of the young child's creative art work (as well as the conceptual understandings, attitudes, motor skills and other factors which it often reveals and upon which it is usually based) varies greatly from one or two to four or five years of age. The nature of the art work of one-, two-, three-, and sometimes four-year-olds depends to a considerable extent upon the amount and kind of their previous art experiences, but it is usually characterized by scribbles and irregular shapes. At the earliest stages of his artistic development, the child tends not to title his works and he rarely attempts to draw or model persons or objects; but he sometimes playacts through art media, interpreting various rhythmic movements or gestures which he may consciously or unconsciously accompany with related sounds or facial expressions. During periods of creative art expression, the young child is often deeply absorbed. Though proof is not yet available, it is believed that such moments of deep interest and concentration coincide with conceptual enrichment and artistic growth.

At three or four years of age, a few children will begin to use pictorial symbols in their art work, some of which may be recognizable by adults. The use of expressive symbols is especially characteristic of children who have been given frequent opportunities for creative art expression during their earliest years and have progressed from the level of play to a level of more specific intent and more highly developed conceptual and expressive ability. Some of the art symbols used by young children are unquestionably imitative of those they have seen in the works of other children, adults, or artists who make illustrations for books, magazines, television, and animated motion pictures, but most are original. Their resemblance to symbols used by other children at similar developmental levels is regarded as a coincidence.

Certainly the frequent appearance in a young child's work of an elliptical shape for a head, horizontal lines for a mouth, with arms and sometimes legs (but seldom a body) connected directly to the head, is an expression of his personal concept of the human figure rather than an imitation of someone else's work. So, too, many other symbols which appear in the young child's art work are believed to be expressions of his inner concepts of persons and objects rather than results of his attempts to portray their actual appearance. The aim in contributing to the development of the young child's art expression should, therefore, be one of conceptual enrichment rather than instruction on how to draw or model subjects in specific ways. Such enrichment appears to be best fostered indirectly by providing appropriate stimuli and art experiences through which the child's conceptual development, expressive skills, and overall interest in creative work seem to evolve naturally.

One remarkable characteristic of the art work of most very young children is its extremely high aesthetic quality. The child appears to have an inherent sense of color, shape, line, and texture which often achieves an overall aesthetic level of professional quality. Part of this phenomenon appears attributable to the aesthetic beauty of the human body and its normal movement patterns. The curved line created by a pencil held in one's fingers as the hand is moved from a bent-back to a bent-forward position is aesthetically pleasing. So are the lines created by other natural finger, wrist, arm, shoulder, and body movements. Part of this high aesthetic quality is believed to result from the young child's inherent sense of design and the tendency of his early concepts to reduce various subjects to their structural and ideological essence. Einstein believed children have an inherent ability to understand advanced mathematical concepts: this inherent ability is likely to extend to art concepts and expressive abilities as well. The problem which vexes art teachers, as it must teachers of mathematics, is how to maintain and build upon this high level of conceptualization and expression. Incidentally, more than a few professional artists have striven (some with success) to recapture in their own art work the beauty of childlike, natural body movements and unfettered conceptual processes.

Art Education in the Primary Grades

It is essential that the primary school child be given adequate opportunities for creative art expression and for the study of professional works of art. His natural facility in art expression and his inherent ability to perceive and even to comment intelligently upon aesthetic qualities in professional art works are hardly adequate reasons for delaying specialized art instruction until the third or fourth grade where he may seem to need more help. On the contrary, modern educational philosophy asks that we help each individual to become all he is capable of becoming. We need to build upon and enrich children's native gifts at the earliest possible age. Certainly, educators must not wait until a child's conceptual or expressive abilities are diminished before offering him aid in the form of specialized instruction. There is, in addition, good reason to believe that more highly developed conceptual and expressive abilities would enable children to pass, with a greater frequency of success, the barrier to further art development which seems to develop during the intermediate grades.

Current professional opinion, including that of leading theorists of elementary education, maintains that no less than one fifth of the total curriculum from kindergarten through Grade 3 be devoted to art! Not often specified, however, is the need to include in a program of primary grade art instruction a period of time for the study of original art works, reproductions, and slides which should be carefully selected and presented in meaningful sequences.

The primary school child needs and wants skillfully guided, carefully planned, frequent, and regular opportunities for creative art expression and for study of works of art. He also needs and wants help in overcoming his natural tendency to imitate and copy, and to work at the leisurely pace of his current ability level rather than at the more challenging (and actually more enjoyable and rewarding) instructional level which a competent art teacher or unusually well-informed classroom teacher can help him reach. Through art, the child learns to visualize, clarify, and enrich the many new concepts introduced to him in the primary grades. He also gains confidence in and derives considerable pleasure from his ability to produce work which satisfies him as well as his teacher.

The teacher's role in the art instruction of primary grade children ranges from friendly encouragement of pupils' art expression to illustrated presentations of art history. Although the primary school child enjoys experimenting with various art materials, he occasionally requires specific suggestions as to their use and he may need help in selecting subjects to illustrate, model, or construct. The art or classroom teacher should do everything possible to encourage children to solve their own problems of conception and expression, yet she should do more than merely say "Draw (or paint or model) anything you wish" or "Do another." She should, whenever possible, talk with individual pupils about subjects which interest them, and guide them, through subtle suggestions, toward developing means of expressing and interpreting their ideas in art forms. She should occasionally give specific advice on ways of achieving ever-higher levels of performance in art expression and offer information on means of improving color, texture, shape relationships, composition, technique, means of expression, media, and the delineation of essential aspects of subjects chosen for interpretation.

In presenting elements of art history, the teacher should concen-

trate upon developing her pupils' knowledge of basic aesthetic principles, such as the artist's means of and success in interpreting
various subjects; the quality of color and shape relationships, composition, proportion emphasis, and balance; and the overall effect.
The teacher might start with historical periods or styles which are
especially appealing to children and which may be related to other
school subjects being studied. Children in primary school usually
enjoy an introductory study of prehistoric, Egyptian, Mycenaean,
Etruscan, medieval, early Renaissance, primitive, or modern art
works. Young children are often attracted to and effectively motivated by certain works by artists such as Appel, Klee, Matisse,
Miro, Nay, Picasso, Rouault, and Rousseau.

Although the provision of appealing art materials such as tempera, brushes, paper, or clay and construction materials is sometimes sufficient as an initial stimulus for creative art expression, the
primary school child should frequently receive special motivation
in the form of dramatic presentations; recorded music or stories
which he might wish to interpret through illustration; slides and
films; pantomimes; puppet shows; field trips to a firehouse, museum,
farm, zoo, or factory; a special observation trip to the playground;
and live animals, reptiles, and unusual objects brought to school.

Many children of five and six and most children of seven and
eight are interested in and can handle almost every art medium and
activity a teacher can introduce. The primary school child must be
cautioned against believing "I've done that, so I don't need to do it
again." He must learn that the subject he selects and the way he
interprets and refines it in paint or chalk is of far greater importance
than his previous familiarity with a particular medium. But as he
progresses through the primary grades he does become interested
in more complex and more challenging art activities such as lino-
leum-block and silkscreen printing; tempera paint applied over
crayon (called "crayon resist" or "crayon batique"); constructions
of wood, metal, and plastic; monoprinting (tempera or oil painting
on glass on which absorbent paper is temporarily pressed); weav-
ing; appliqué wall hangings; and textile designs. In picture-making
and sculpture he enjoys solving such problems as mixing colors,
achieving compositional balance, constructing armatures, and cre-
ating texture. By the time he is seven or eight he is ready for (but

requires careful safety precautions and supervision in) carving sandstone, printing with oil-base inks, and using sharp-pointed scissors to make detailed cutout designs and paper sculptures.

The paintings, sculpture, collages, and other art works produced by primary grade children, especially when there is a free selection of subject, tend to be pleasant interpretations of themes which are usually recognizable to adults. With rare exceptions, the five- to eight-year-old's work is naively charming, attractive in color and texture, effectively composed, and carefully executed. The child of six, seven, or eight can choose (or even be asked to portray) almost any subject or theme. He will usually begin to draw or model without hesitation, and in twenty or thirty minutes will produce a beautifully simplified, usually well-designed interpretation. He frequently reduces a complex mechanism (such as a tractor) to its most essential components and may enlarge or emphasize by means of color or texture those parts which he believes to be of particular importance.

Though the child's art expression becomes increasingly less spontaneous as he grows older, he continues to produce art works of surprisingly high aesthetic quality through seven, eight, or even nine or ten years of age. He will, for example, more or less automatically locate a tree, a person, a house, a bird, an abstract design element, or a lump of clay in what the professional artist might call the "perfect" spot in a given composition. He will, with apparent ease and speed, decide on (and apply) colors which appear to equal the lyric beauty of those used by a Chagall, a Redon, or a Matisse. He will, with obvious ease, fashion shapes of clay which closely approximate the beautifully proportioned relationships found in a Lipchitz or a Giacometti. Like the work of preschool children, the art products of five- to eight-year-olds appeal to professional artists who recognize the power and beauty of direct, unspoiled creative expression and aesthetic insight. But without highly skilled and frequent guidance during these years of art educational development, and particularly during the intermediate school years which follow, most children will soon face seemingly insurmountable obstacles in creative expression which will cause them to abandon, at least to curtail, their interest in painting, modeling, construction, and related activities.

Art Education in the Intermediate Grades

Between the ages of eight and twelve, most children go through an artistic crisis. During this period, most of them reach a stage of intelligence and perceptual power which causes a conflict between their current level of art expressive ability and what they have come to know as reality. Unless they have been receiving specialized art instruction, they often become dissatisfied—even frustrated—by their inability to draw and paint things as they "really" look. They often abandon further attempts at creative art expression, shielding their disappointment with such typical remarks as "I'm not an artist," "I can't even draw a straight line," or "Art is kid stuff." During these years, the child's need for highly skilled guidance in creative expression is probably greater than at any other phase of his life.

But while the child's art expression usually founders during this period (and may do so, temporarily, even with skilled art instruction), his aesthetic sensitivity to and knowledge of the arts will, if proper learning experiences are provided, continue to make substantial and lasting gains. The wise teacher realizes that although the child's increasing intelligence and perceptivity causes him temporary difficulty in art expression, the same characteristics facilitate the development of art knowledge.

As much as nine tenths of the time in the art curriculum of intermediate grade children was once devoted to art expression, primarily in drawing with crayons, painting with watercolors, and working in related media. Whatever time remained may have been used for art appreciation. The ways in which both aspects of traditional art education programs were handled and the amount of time given to each are now looked upon with disfavor. Modern art educational theory, based on extensive successful practices and considerable research, recommends that approximately one third of the time in the intermediate grade art program be used for each of the following: guided creative expression in drawing, painting, and other two-dimensional media; guided creative expression in the crafts, sculpture, collage, and other three-dimensional media; and guided study of professional art works in painting, sculpture, architecture, community planning, and related fields. Under ideal circumstances (recommended by elementary educators as well as art educators), as much as one fifth of the entire elementary school program would be given to art education, the responsibility for which would obviously need to be shared by art teachers and classroom teachers—the former providing general guidance, encouragement, time, and materials for supplemental and correlated art activities. With such an appropriately generous allocation of time, it is possible—through art education—to change the intermediate grade years from a period of crisis to one of fruitful and pleasurable growth.

The role of the art teacher and—to the extent of her capabilities—that of the classroom teacher in the art education of eight- to twelve-year-olds continues, as in the primary grades, to be one of friendly encouragement and skillful instructional guidance. But intermediate grade pupils often need and request more help in conceptualization and technique than do younger children. To neglect such individual needs is unwise, even unethical. A few teachers still believe (wrongly) that specific art instruction is contrary to the prevailing philosophy of creative art teaching. Others complain that too many or too large classes preclude even occasional individualized teaching, not realizing that three or four minutes per week of intensive personal attention to a pupil's needs may be more beneficial than one or two hours of group instruction. A compromise practice of dividing instructional time between groups and individuals is satisfactory in most instances. The skillful teacher, in fact, often utilizes both methods during a single lesson period, regardless of the size or number of classes. The pupil who asks how to draw, paint, or model a particular subject is first asked to try to portray it to the best of his ability. He is then asked to tell all he knows about it and may be provided with others' verbal descriptions, or photographs, slides, actual objects, films, and reproductions of art works. He may then be asked to portray the subject in question again, incorporating (but not copying) into the new version as much as possible of what has been said and shown.

When requested to do so or when she feels it desirable, the art teacher of intermediate grade children may occasionally demonstrate several ways of conceptualizing and portraying subjects of interest. She would probably not, however, leave the work where it might be copied, nor would she encourage pupils to draw, paint, or model things in this way. She would encourage pupils to observe carefully and think about subjects which interest them, to utilize reference materials (such as her demonstrations, other artists' works, photographs, and so forth) sensitively, intelligently, and honestly. She would urge them to develop personalized concepts and techniques, just as she and other artists have done. She would discourage, but not forbid or ridicule, imitating and copying. She would praise original work, especially that produced by pupils whose earlier efforts had been dependent on the concepts and techniques of others.

The teacher strives to achieve a sensible balance between her demonstrations of new processes and techniques and free experimentation by pupils. She realizes the value of personal discovery in technique but she also knows that this is usually less important than the development of a personal style of expression, less significant than the refinement of conceptualization, less valuable than the quality of subject interpretation, and less meaningful than the attainment of total aesthetic excellence. With potentially dangerous tools and processes—such as pointed scissors and tools for wire sculpture, block-cutting, and etching—she takes no chances: she carefully demonstrates their correct use, states precautions, and strictly enforces safety regulations.

Most of the stimuli suggested for use at the primary school level (see p. 64) can, with appropriate modifications, be used in the intermediate grades as well. A few, however, are unusually effective with children who are more mature and peer-oriented in their interests and whose intelligence and perceptive powers are more highly developed. Among these stimuli are outdoor sketching trips to zoos, boatyards, farms, and factories; educational television and radio programs; art games (such as one in which each child in turn places one line or shape on a marked-off section of the blackboard in a group effort to create an excellent design or humorous illustration, or a version of Twenty Questions on art history topics); playbacks of sound effects or discussions tape-recorded by pupils; pupil-created dramatic skits and pantomimes; and the mere mention that a new art medium or activity is complicated and difficult. A great number of professional art works possess powerful motivating qualities, inspiring pupils to acquire knowledge of their style and content and subsequently to produce their own art work.

Among artists of the past who have produced certain works which are likely to have special appeal at this age level are Bruegel, Crivelli, Degas, Delacroix, Holbein, Michelangelo, Rembrandt, Signorelli, and Turner. Many contemporary painters, sculptors, architects, and community designers, if carefully chosen with the age level interests of pupils in mind, would provide deep stimuli. Among these are Bellows, Brancusi, Chagall, Corbusier, Dali, Max Ernst, Morris Graves, Picasso, Tamayo, and Frank Lloyd Wright.

Children in the eight- to twelve-year-old range have such extensive interests and abilities and in many respects are so versatile, competent, and eager for challenging experiences that it might be more appropriate to ask "With what materials, tools, processes, and activities is the art teacher or classroom teacher familiar?" rather than present so extensive a list as that which follows in Table 2.[5] The art teacher or classroom teacher can do no more than choose from this wide assortment those activities, processes, and techniques with which he is or is willing to become familiar. But the intermediate grade child who has proper instruction, materials, tools, and a place to work can engage in most art activities with comparative ease.

Not included in Table 2 is the study of professional art works which should represent at least one third of the art education curriculum at this level. Examples—originals whenever possible—of the finest painting, sculpture, architecture, community planning, the crafts, photography, the graphic arts, and applied design should be systematically studied, with emphasis being placed upon the development of aesthetically oriented value judgments and the acquisition of stylistic, technical, historic, and sociological information concerning the works and periods studied.

Jerome S. Bruner presents a theory applicable to the study of art in the intermediate grades:

> If one respects the ways of thought of the growing child, if one is courteous enough to translate material into his logical forms and challenging enough to tempt him to advance, then it is possible to introduce him at an early age to the ideas and styles that in later life make an educated man.[6]

---

[5] Adapted from Howard Conant and Arne Randall, *Art in Education* (Peoria, Ill.: Chas. A. Bennett Co., Inc., 1963), pp. 136–37.

[6] Jerome S. Bruner, *The Process of Education* (Cambridge, Mass.: Harvard University Press, 1961), p. 52.

TABLE 2

Art Media, Tools, Techniques, and Activities Suggested for Children in the Eight to Eleven-Year-Old Age Range *

	Paper and Cardboard	Clay and Plaster	Wire and Metal	Wood

Tools and Techniques	Cut
	  scissors,
	  stencil knife
	  paper cutter
	Tear
	Crumple
	Fold
	Weave
	Roll
	Paste
	Model (paper mâché)
	Assemble (cardboard boxes)
		Squeeze
		Punch
		Pull
		Press
		Cut in strips
		  (attach with slip)
		Glaze
		Fire
		Carve
		Model
		Pour in self-designed cast of plaster or sand
			Cut
			Bend
			Pinch
			Twist
			Solder
			Fasten
			Pound
			Turn
			Polish
			Heat
			Cool
			Weld
			Braze
				Saw
				Build
				Nail
				Carve
				Turn
				Use in collage
				Assemble with other scrap materials

Types of Activities or Objects	Puppets
	Paper sculpture
	Booklets
	Masks
	Shoe box "theaters"
	Murals
	Painting
	Printing
	Holiday ornaments
	Mâché modeling
	Cleaning bag costumes
	Party hats
	Pasted strips construction
	  figures
	  animals
	  rhythm instruments
	  totem poles
	  kite-making
		Animals
		Figures
		Bowls
		Candle holders
		Pin trays
		Dishes
		Earrings
		Pins
		Ash trays
		Vases
		Plaster/string spheres
		  (over inflated balloons)
		Plastic (oil base)
		  clay modeling
		Sawdust with wallpaper paste
		Clay with grog, sand or pebbles
		Mosaic wall hangings, trays
			Wire sculpture
			Mobile
			Stabiles
			Scrap material sculpture
			Dishes, trays
			Spatter printing (with wire screen, toothbrush)
			Sculpture
			  steel
			  brass
			  copper
			  iron
				Furniture
				Toys
				Wheels
				Masts for boats
				Looms
				Armatures
				Sculpture
				  carved
				  toothpick
				  scrap wood
				  driftwood
				Stage sets

	String, Yarn, Rope, Reed	Textiles	Print Media	Tempera, Watercolor, Oil Paint	Crayon and Chalk
Tools and Techniques	Weave spools tongue depressors looms Navajo box cardboard Knit Crochet Hook rugs Stich by hand or machines	Sew by hand or machine Stencil crayon tempera lacquer shellac textile paint	Cutting and engraving celluloid copper zinc silk glass rubber Stencil knife scissors hammer and tacks	Paint with flat, pointed, bristle, sable, or camel hair brushes Stencil	Draw (point, side) Etch Melt Rub over textured surfaces Combine with watercolor, tempera
Types of Activities or Objects	Weaving scarves, rugs, mats Knitting scarves, socks, sweaters Hooking, rugs, wall Stitching, appliqué designs Basketry	Wall hangings Toys Puppets Doll costumes Purses Boat sails Wigwams Rag dolls Decorative banners for school festivals parades	Printing linoleum woodcut vegetable stick sponge inner tube Monoprinting Etching Silkscreening	Finger painting Murals Designs Pictures Portfolio covers Stenciling Tempera-over-crayon Posters and signs	Designs Figures Sketching Murals Posters Stenciling greeting cards place mats Crayon etching Chalk on wet bogus paper

* This list of art media and activities represents only a portion of those which are appropriate for this and certain other interest and ability levels. Although children in the eight to eleven-year-old range are able to handle sharp tools, they need close supervision, preferably in groups of six to eight.

But to *translate material into the child's logical form* does not mean to present it superficially as has been done in teaching "art appreciation" to children. It means, instead, that art teachers and classroom teachers should present works of art and information concerning them in as original and complete a form as possible. Because his intelligence and perceptivity have developed further, the child at this age level is capable of grasping advanced aesthetic concepts. He is also capable of grappling with real ideas, genuine issues, and hard facts—some of them unpleasant, complex, open-ended, intimate, or unpopular. Clearly, the history of art is richly laden with ideas and styles which, if introduced to the child in understandable terms, will *in later life make an educated man.* If the ideal allocation of one fifth of the total elementary school curriculum to art education can be widely attained, two forty-five minute periods per week could be devoted to the study of works of art. Augmented by four other forty-five minute periods (or the equivalent) per week for creative art expression, such instruction could, within the normal span of elementary school years, contribute with amazing effectiveness to the art knowledge, critical judgment, and expressive ability of future adults.

The drawings and paintings (especially if they are representational) produced by children of intermediate school years are—both in actual aesthetic quality and in the way they are regarded by their creators—generally inferior to their abstract two-dimensional works, craft objects, sculptures, and applied designs. This is primarily due to a self-recognized discrepancy between what a child sees and knows and what he is able to draw and paint. But, especially at the beginning of this age range, children do occasionally produce representational works of aesthetic beauty. With rare exceptions which are probably induced by poor or uncreative teaching, most of the art work of intermediate grade children is good in overall art quality, sincere, naively charming, effectively composed, attractively proportioned, and more or less original in concept and technique. And it can be raised to a higher level of quality through constructive criticism by an art teacher.

The child of eight still uses symbols (the same design for a house may appear in his work many times with only slight modifications) and concepts (such as the base line of ground upon which all pictorial elements are securely placed) which are actually more characteristic of children in the primary grades. But by the time he is twelve, he will, in most cases, have stopped producing what appear to him to be childish works, and he will (if he was lucky enough to have had skilled art educational guidance) be interpreting what he observes in an artistic format of increasing aesthetic quality (especially in sculpture, the crafts, and printing). He will, on even more rare occasions, once again try to produce a personally satisfying work, but, noting its resemblance to those of his earlier childhood, will probably once again resolve to give up creative expression in art.

But all pupils throughout the intermediate school years are as easily capable of developing a sound and fairly extensive knowledge of their art heritage, past and present, as they are of learning to understand literature and other major disciplines. To acquire this vital knowledge of man's culture, they should receive appropriate instruction from a teacher of art as well as from their classroom teachers. Classroom teachers should be prepared to teach the subject matter of the arts just as they teach social studies and the sciences, whether or not they have available the services of a specialist teacher in each area.

Art Education in Youth Groups, Religious Training, and Summer Camps

Ideally, a separate section on nonschool art education programs would be unnecessary, since the best aspects of youth groups, summer camps, religious groups, museums, mass communication media, and public and private school art educational activities would be mutually adopted, and only the various settings, media, and times of day or year in which programs of art education were presented would need to be described.

But as matters now stand, programs of art education in youth groups, religious groups, and summer camps are often vastly different from (and usually inferior to) those found in most public and private elementary and secondary schools and in museums; hence, special, essentially remedial, treatment in this separate section is necessary.

For numerous and often baffling or contradictory reasons, and in the good names of social work, outdoor education, and religion, most of the art activities carried on by organizations in these fields are stereotyped, needlessly expensive, either meaningless or actually harmful, and poorly oriented to the concepts held by their leaders. The low quality of the art programs in youth groups, Sunday schools, and summer camps is probably due primarily to the fact that most of the persons who provide art activity leadership in these organizations are not properly trained as teachers of art but are, instead, low-paid high school or college students, or adult volunteers. Furthermore, the administrators of these groups have usually received little or no art education, and although they are vitally concerned with individual human welfare and do much to promote it, they unknowingly permit—even encourage—their personnel to guide children in "art" activities which induce conformity, discourage creative thought and action, waste time, cost too much money, are often frustrating, stress copying, and foster dishonest pride in finished-looking products which have been designed by someone else and merely assembled by the child. All too familiar are the pseudo-Indian leather (now plastic) purses, "gimp" lanyards and key chains, ovenbaked (or self-hardening clay) ash trays, painted-by-numbers pictures, outlined pictures of religious subjects which children are to "color in," and endless other objects which are produced by the tens of thousands each year in American youth groups, Sunday schools, and summer camps. The only persons who benefit from these noncreative, time-consuming, and probably harmful activities are the manufacturers of kits and other "arts and crafts" materials who are making lots of money at the expense of children's imaginations. Like producers of inferior motion pictures, they try to excuse themselves by pleading that they are merely meeting a public demand. In the case of youth groups, Sunday schools, and summer camps, the "demand" comes from innocent, well-meaning, but poorly art-educated administrators, leaders, teachers, and counselors who fall prey to the your-children-will-love-it and anyone-can-do-it advertisements of unscrupulous art materials firms. To combat this problem, an increasing number of art educators today are:

1. Conferring with, writing for, lecturing to, and teaching classes for administrators, leaders, teachers, and counselors of youth groups, religious organizations, and summer camps in order to acquaint them with ways in which their art activities may be made compatible with both the

highest aims of art education and the expressed purposes of recreation, religious education, or camping;

2. Securing positions in these organizations as art activity leaders, teachers, counselors, or program directors;

3. Urging fellow art teachers as well as youth group, religious organization, and summer camp personnel not to purchase art materials from companies which manufacture kits, devices, or materials which are considered undesirable or harmful by the art education profession;

4. Including the long-neglected problems of art education in youth groups, religious organizations, and summer camps in their talks to parent-teacher associations and other groups, in their college art education courses, and in their writing.

The role of the art teacher, leader, or counselor in youth groups, Sunday schools, or summer camps should be nearly identical to his role in elementary or secondary schools, except for possible differences in dress and demeanor. The mere fact that participants are known as members of an art club, craft group, Sunday school class, or camp instead of as pupils in a school does not call for a role change on the part of the teacher, nor does their choice of special subjects or materials call for stereotyped or directed teaching instead of creative and aesthetically oriented art teaching. As a matter of fact, the frequently longer time periods, proportionately larger allocation of funds, informal working conditions, and voluntary attendance offer possibilities for a strengthened role for the imaginative teacher of art.

What has been said about the teaching of art in elementary and secondary schools applies, at appropriate age levels, to the art programs of youth groups, Sunday schools, and summer camps. But there are certain stimuli and activities, in addition to those which have been described, which are particularly well-suited to the programs of these organizations. In youth groups, for example, one might expect leaders to facilitate cooperative activities among groups working in art, music, drama, and the dance. The frequency and long time spans which characterize the youth group participation of many youngsters makes it possible, for example, to concentrate upon the planning, writing, designing, staging, performance, and evaluation of a theatrical production which might be difficult to fit into the programs of many schools. Sunday school teachers might ask pupils to paint their impression of Biblical themes, utilizing stained glass windows, organ music, and child-level interpretations of weekly lessons as stimuli. Sunday school teachers should discontinue the use of adult-designed, fill-in pictures and other stereotyped materials. Summer camp counselors might suggest creative uses for pebbles, sticks, leaves, bark, and reeds, and might use films, stories, and articles on the Indians and other primitive cultures as stimuli. They should discourage the making of stereotyped camp souvenirs and should discontinue the use of predesigned craft and painting kits.

The comparative flexibility of youth group and summer camp schedules, and the many stimuli inherent in their environments as well as in those of Sunday schools, make it possible to offer creative art programs of the highest caliber as part of the activities in these nonschool organizations—art programs which should enrich and supplement the expressed fundamental aims of these groups. But the introduction of significant creative art activities into the program of youth groups, Sunday schools, and summer camps necessitates recognition of their importance by the administrators of such organizations, and the hiring of competent art specialists as leaders, teachers, and counselors.

Art Education for Exceptional Children

Children who differ markedly from their peers in mental, physical, emotional, or social characteristics are generally classified as *exceptional* and may have special art educational needs. Under ideal circumstances, their special needs are met by trained experts, but their total educational development is integrated as closely as possible into the normal environmental conditions of school, home, and community.

Except for the gifted children, exceptional children were, in the past, usually isolated from their normal peer groups. Perhaps inadvertently, but often cruelly, handicapped individuals were treated in ways which emphasized, rather than alleviated, their deficiencies. Modern educational theory, based on extensive research, stresses the needs of exceptional children to be related as fully as possible to normal individuals of similar age and interests.

The nature of art work which exceptional children can produce and the art concepts they are capable of developing are as widely varied as those of other groups. It is of utmost importance for parents, classroom teachers, art teachers, and specialists in the fields of medicine, social work, and psychology to bear the following principles in mind:

1. Children with special mental, physical, or social problems are often as able to express themselves artistically and to understand the arts as other children are.

2. Children who are intellectually or otherwise (e.g., musically) gifted are not necessarily gifted in art, and vice versa.

3. Children believed to be artistically gifted may not become artistically talented adults.

Art education for the gifted. Giftedness in creative art expression and the ability to understand the arts is difficult to evaluate, particularly at the elementary school level. Even later, what is believed to be giftedness may turn out to be mere facility. Rapid expression and quick understanding in the arts are not necessarily reliable indices of profound quality or extensive scope. A number of factors make the determination of giftedness in art a predominantly subjective matter: lack of specific information on artistic giftedness; the inherent ability of most primary and many intermediate grade children to produce art work of high aesthetic quality and to grasp the fundamentals of artistic criticism; the unreliability of tests designed to measure art expression or judgment; and the highly variable nature of art itself. The best present advice on this matter for the conscientious teacher, parent, or counselor is to provide each child with the fundamental art education recommended for his grade or age level, plus as many more advanced art experiences as his interest and ability and the resources of his community, school, and home will permit.

Elementary and secondary schools should sponsor art clubs for children who show special interest and ability in this area. Advanced instruction might also be provided in special classes sponsored by the school or by a community art museum or youth group. Special care should be taken to guide children who are believed to be artistically gifted into classes taught by competent, creative art teachers, rather than into classes taught by those who have little or no qualification beyond a desire to earn extra income. Elementary and secondary school art teachers, college art teachers, and teachers of museum art classes are usually the best available judges of children's giftedness. Parents, relatives, classroom teachers, amateur artists, and peers are seldom qualified judges of artistic giftedness. They often mistake giftedness for normal art ability, especially at the early childhood level.

Among the experiences which qualified art teachers might offer children believed to be gifted in the creation or study of art are studio experiences in unfamiliar media or processes such as oil painting, wood engraving, silkscreen printing, pastel drawing, stone carving, self-designed auto or airplane model construction, and the planning and building of stage sets. Artistically gifted children might also enjoy and profit from receiving writing assignments on artists' lives, researching the origins of a design form such as the chair, filling a sketch book with drawings of different varieties of trees or animals, and reporting on special visits to art galleries or museums. The artistically gifted child desires and should receive frank, detailed, and constructive criticism on his creative and written work. He welcomes praise when he feels it is deserved, but he desires much more than routine approval of his work.

The development of the talents of artistically gifted children is as important to the future of civilization as the identification and training of potential leaders in science, mathematics, and other fields. It is imperative for all children to receive at least a fundamental education in the arts. Once this basic aim has been achieved, as it has in many American schools, the identification of children believed to be artistically gifted will be greatly enhanced, and the need to offer regularly scheduled, advanced art classes at all educational levels will be more clearly realized.

Art education for children with special mental, physical, or social problems. Children who are mentally retarded, deaf or hard of hearing, blind or with partial sight, otherwise physically handicapped, or socially maladjusted require the aid of trained psychological, medical, and social work personnel and agencies as well as that of parents and teachers who understand their special needs and attempt to meet them. Art plays an especially important role in the education, and often in the rehabilitation, of these children. Through art activities, many children, adolescents, and even adults who fall into one or more of these special problem areas have derived not only pleasure but conceptual enrichment and increased expressive ability as well. Furthermore, they have—usually under the cooperative guidance of an art teacher, medical and psychological specialists, and regular teachers of exceptional pupils—derived such therapeutic benefits as improved coordination; strengthened (or relaxed) muscles; calmed (or released) emotions; increased personal satisfaction; feelings of greater security; heightened perception of colors, shapes, textures, light and dark values, and detail; improved social relationships; and deepened understanding of concepts in other subjects.

Nearly all the art activities and processes recommended for the various elementary and secondary school grade groupings (see pp. 58–73 and pp. 81–85) can be profitably enjoyed by youngsters with special mental, physical, or social problems. In many cases, however, art media and processes need to be adapted to the specific needs of various types of exceptional children on the basis of information secured through consultation with medical, psychological, educational, and social work specialists.

Art Education in Secondary Schools

The emphasis in American secondary school art education has been and continues to be placed upon students' creative expression in drawing, painting, sculpture, and various types of applied design. But although creative expression is valuable for persons at all age levels and necessary for the development of an adequate understanding of the arts, it is not now regarded by leading art educators as being of primary importance in the general secondary education of American youth. Some art educators now recommend that as much as two thirds of the secondary school art program be devoted to the development of students' understanding of the finest historic and contemporary examples of painting, sculpture, architecture, community planning, the crafts, photography, and applied design. They view the secondary school art program as one which should be primarily oriented to the educational needs of general, rather than specialized, students. They recommend that as many as four consumer-oriented courses in art be required of all students in Grades 7, 8, 9 or 10, and 11 or 12. The additional needs of students preparing for art careers would be met through specialized elective courses in Grades 9–12. The implementation of these recommendations will necessitate a virtual reversal in present art educational practices and course requirements in American secondary schools.

It is imperative for the sake of individual students and in the interests of the society of which they will soon be adult members that the aforementioned changes in emphasis in secondary school art education be implemented without further delay.

Art plays an increasingly important role in modern life. The quality of every manufactured product, every home and apartment, and every community is determined by the nature of its design. The high school student and, later, the adult who does not possess a knowledge of the aesthetic bases of fine as well as applied art is at an economic disadvantage as well as at an artistic disadvantage. All young people, not just the well-to-do or the lucky few who happen to attend schools with consumer-oriented required art courses, need and are entitled to a comprehensive art education of the highest quality. The already tremendous and ever-increasing scope of the arts, which affects practically every aspect of our lives, makes it as important for students to learn the visual language and content of the arts as it is for them to learn the language and content of literature.

These urgently needed changes in secondary school art education necessitate drastic modifications in the traditional roles of junior and senior high school art teachers. No longer can they function primarily as studio masters, spending most of their time guiding students' creative expression in drawing, painting, and occasional three-dimensional media. No longer can they stress their favorite art school subject, such as mask-making, watercolor painting, or copper enameling, neglecting the development of their students' overall art knowledge. No longer can art teachers regard youngsters in their classes as youthful prototypes of art school students. The role which art education now asks junior and senior high school art teachers to assume will be one which is more scholarly, initially less appealing, less dramatic, and more time-demanding; but, eventually, it will be seen to be rewarding both to themselves and to their students.

To prepare for his new role, the secondary school art teacher will need additional courses in the history of art, and more than the usual amount of sociology, history, psychology, and literature. His studio course work will probably require little, if any, supplementation, unless he has specialized in one medium. In his study of art history, sociology, and history, he will need to learn the aesthetic fundamentals, historical contexts, and sociological bases of major art works, periods, and styles. He must be familiar with painting, sculpture, and architecture, and with applied design as well. It would be difficult to acquire such knowledge by means of independent study or with less than thirty-five credit hours of college course work in art history and liberal arts subjects.

In presenting the vast subject matter of the visual and plastic arts to his students, the secondary school art teacher will need to select examples which are representative of much more which cannot be shown; to make extensive use of slides, art books, films, educational television, reproductions, filmstrips, and original art works; to plan and conduct field trips; to secure guest speakers for his classes and for school assembly programs; and to consider carefully the interests and intellectual capacities of his students. There is no reason why secondary school art courses cannot be as interesting—and as valuable—to students as the finest courses in history and literature; in fact, the tangible, visual nature of the arts make them appealing and comparatively easy for most students to comprehend. The art teacher should make chronological, thematic, or otherwise well-organized and illustrated presentations of art works, periods, and styles. He should require students to take notes in class and to maintain an illustrated notebook. He should allow time for discussion and conduct studio activities designed to enrich students' learning experiences in the study of art as well as to develop their personal expressive powers. And, finally, he should give homework assignments in reading, creative work, and museum visiting.

Among the studio work experiences in which the junior and senior high school student should participate are creative painting, sculpture, and modeling, which will help him better understand the styles, techniques, and content of professional works he is studying. In addition to these experiences which, indeed, have dominated secondary art education but were seldom related to the development of students' understanding of the works of professional artists, there is a need for introductory studio work in clothing design, the crafts, photography, interior design, architecture, furniture design, community planning, and advertising design. However, since the emphasis in secondary school art education should be placed upon a study of, rather than personal creative experiences in, these art fields, it is necessary that the time devoted to each be appropriately divided

TABLE 3

SUGGESTED DIVISION OF SECONDARY SCHOOL EXPERIENCES IN REQUIRED ART COURSES *

Grade 7	Grade 8	Grade 9 or 10	Grade 11 or 12
Crafts Study of contemporary and historic pottery, textiles, and jewelry: 50 hrs. Studio experiences in pottery-making (coil, slab, and wheel), textile designing, simple jewelry-making: 30 hrs. *Painting, Sculpture, and Graphic Arts* Study of selected major works from prehistoric to modern times: 50 hrs. Related studio experiences: 30 hrs. *Textile and Clothing Design* Study of historic and contemporary examples: 25 hrs. Related studio experiences: 15 hrs.	*Graphic Arts* Study of historic and contemporary works in woodcut, lithographic, and linoleum print media: 15 hrs. Studio work in linoleum and wood cutting and printing: 15 hrs. *Architecture* Study of major historic and contemporary works: 15 hrs. Studio work in designing an ideal school or community building: 10 hrs. *Community Planning* Study of major historic and contemporary examples: 15 hrs. Studio work in design of an ideal community: 10 hrs. *Painting and Sculpture* Study of major modern (1850 to present) works: 40 hrs. Studio experience in styles inspired by modern artists: 30 hrs. *Commercial Design* Study of examples of advertising and product design: 25 hrs. Studio experiences in design: 25 hrs.	*Photography* Study of major historic and contemporary photographs: 30 hrs. Studio and field work in photography, including darkroom procedures: 20 hrs. *Textile and Clothing Design* Study of historic and contemporary examples: 30 hrs. Related studio experiences: 20 hrs. *Industrial Design* Study of professional examples of furniture, appliance, and automotive design: 20 hrs. Related studio experiences: 10 hrs. *Painting, Sculpture and Graphic Arts* Study of major historic and contemporary works: 40 hrs. Related studio experiences: 30 hrs.	*Community Planning* Study of Niemeyer's "Brasilia," Corbusier's "Chandigarh," Mies Van Der Rohe, and others, and designs by Gruen: 30 hrs. Studio experiences in designing an ideal community, a cultural center, or replanning the local community: 20 hrs. *Architecture* Study of works by Wright, Corbusier, Mies Van Der Rohe, Gropius, Breuer, Skidmore-Owings-Merrill, Harrison and Abramovitz, and others: 50 hrs. Studio experiences in designing a home: 20 hrs. *Painting, Sculpture and Graphic Arts* Study of major historic and contemporary works: 40 hrs. Studio experience in oil and watercolor painting; clay, stone, and wood sculpture; woodcutting, engraving, and etching: 40 hrs.
Total Hours: 200	*Total Hours:* 200	*Total Hours:* 200	*Total Hours:* 200

* Allocation of time based on four full-year (forty weeks), five-hour-per-week courses required of all students. It is expected that study and studio experiences will be intermingled, rather than offered in block sequences.

throughout Grades 7–12. It would be educationally unwise to attempt to include all these areas in a single art course. The experiences in art study and expression proposed as part of the educational requirements for all secondary school students might be divided as suggested in Table 3.

Not only must the emphasis in secondary school art education be placed upon the study, rather than the practice, of art, but the approach to both needs to be reoriented. Students in secondary school art classes must be recognized, first, as adolescents whose interests and abilities are different from those of children or adults; and, second, as potential consumers, rather than producers, of art. Both as adolescents and as individuals whose art background is extremely limited, they need art experiences which are closely related to their present levels of interest and ability, but which will, in addition, equip them for the many demands upon their art knowledge which will come with adult life.

Both because of his age and background, the adolescent's notion of the meaning of art is more often than not at variance with that of the art teacher. Through upbringing and inadequate education in the arts, he has inherited many of society's prejudices toward modern art: like his parents and other adults, he probably prefers realistic, narrative modes of expression and is particularly interested in works which are romantic in flavor and sensuous in content. To build upon what really interests the adolescent, instead of what he is expected to like, the secondary school art teacher will probably have to begin the study of art at the quality level characteristic of magazine illustrations, popular photography, theater billboards, and home decorating journals. By comparing these with professional art works which use similar techniques but are more profound in style and concept, the art teacher can help students gradually build bases for sound art judgment which, when they are faced with more complex aesthetic problems such as those presented by abstract art, will permit them to respond in a manner which is cultured, sensitive, and intelligent, rather than biased and ill-informed.

Similarly, in aspects of secondary school art courses devoted to pupils' personal art expression, the art teacher will expect to see, and plan to build upon, modes of art expression which are illustrative, stereotyped, and strongly oriented toward typical adolescent interests in self-understanding, the opposite sex, clothing and grooming styles, motor cars, sports, and popular entertainment. If his interest is to be maintained and his best effort encouraged, the secondary school student must be given guidance in portraying subjects which genuinely interest him in styles of interpretation which he prefers. Gradually, he may be led to choose subjects and modes of interpretation which better lend themselves to significance in art.

The secondary school art teacher should also provide students with combined art study and expression experiences in the design of communities, buildings and interiors, tools and appliances, advertisements, clothing, and textiles. Under ideal circumstances, a special room (or a portion of an oversize art room) would serve as a design laboratory where solid geometric and free-shaped forms could be used to create community plans; where building models could be designed and constructed; where actual examples of well-designed furniture and accessories could be studied and arranged in various ways; where the design of actual tools and appliances could be evaluated and perhaps improved; where posters could be designed, pasted up, or printed; where clothing could be designed and made; and where textiles might be woven or printed.

The nature of art work produced by secondary school students ranges from naive to sophisticated, crude to skillful, careless to painstaking, and dull to imaginative. A similarly wide range of ability will be noted in the development of art concepts derived from their art study experiences. Because art courses should be required of all secondary school students and not just for those believed to be talented, the craft objects, pictures, sculptures, and other objects they produce will rarely exhibit outstanding aesthetic quality. For most students, these experiences in creative expression will primarily enhance their understanding of related works of professional art rather than their ability to produce objects of artistic worth. A few students, however, may be expected to produce work of moderate aesthetic excellence. But nearly every secondary school student can develop a good understanding of works produced by professional artists, and some youngsters will gain deep insight into the realm of aesthetics.

The art teacher should encourage those of his students who show special interest or aptitude in the study, practice and/or teaching of art to consider these as possible careers. Especially because art careers are often neglected or downgraded by guidance counselors and parents, art teachers should discuss them briefly in all their classes and should explain them in detail to students who show special interest. Excellent art career literature is now available and should be found in every junior and senior high school art room and guidance office (see Bibliography).

Art in Higher Education

Both the study and practice of art are now well-established disciplines in higher education. A steadily increasing number of schools require all students to take at least one art course as part of their basic education, whether they are majoring in liberal arts or preparing for a specific profession or vocation. Concerning the importance of art in higher education, the late President Griswold of Yale University recently said:

> The rise of the fine arts in the universities has paralleled their rise in the nation to the highest and most promising stage of their development. . . . creative art and higher education are so closely related as to form an integral process. . . . a distinguishing feature of a true university is liberal learning. . . . [It is] one of the university's chief sources of strength and reasons for being. . . . [Creative art] should be treated in a vital relationship to liberal learning. . . .
>
> Another reason why the universities should stand by and strengthen the fine arts is the very one that compels them to strengthen the sciences. We are living in a time when science is being called upon to save our skins before art can save our souls. . . . I am convinced that science alone, unaided by the arts, cannot save us, either as a nation or as a civilization.[6]

And in a highly significant curriculum study published by one of the nation's leading centers for the preparation of scientists and engineers, we are advised:

> Until very recently American educational thinking has tended to disregard the visual arts as a field of universal, practical necessity above the elementary level. Even now the great majority of high school and college students will terminate their formal education without any experience of the visual arts. . . . American education has been, and still is, based on vocational convenience rather than deep-rooted values. . . . As a result, there is a discrepancy between

---

[6] A. Whitney Griswold, "The Fine Arts and the Universities," *Atlantic* (June, 1959), 53–56.

the average freshman's ability to think and to see. Already scholastically mature, he has yet to learn his ABC's in visual terms. . . . an art program can cultivate a feeling for intuitive qualities which cannot be strictly advanced by logic, yet upon which the modern scientist finds himself increasingly dependent.[7]. . .

Leaders in business, industry, and the professions are asking institutions of higher learning to increase course requirements in art and the other humanities, even if this necessitates a reduction in course requirements in the major subject sequence. These leaders quite correctly realize that modern business, industrial, and professional needs are as broadly cultural as they are specialized in orientation. Their interest in enriching the liberal arts backgrounds of incoming personnel is, therefore, as much a result of concern for their special fields as it is a result of belief in the importance of education. Some executives have decided to provide recent college graduates with on-the-job training in lieu of certain undergraduate courses in the major subject (such as engineering) in order that time (and credits) might thus be made available for art and other humanities courses. They have found it easier and, over a period of time, more valuable to do this than to hire persons who are technically or professionally well-trained but who lack the ideological and conceptual foundations which a well-balanced and reasonably complete liberal arts education provides. Modern business, industrial, and professional leaders believe that the best and most valuable decisions will be made by personnel who have a strong background in the liberal arts as well as in their field of specialization. Even the art directors of popular magazines and advertising agencies have asked professional art schools to substitute liberal arts courses for certain advanced technical courses. Among neophyte commercial artists, they prefer those who have had sociologically and historically oriented courses in the study of art to those who took additional technical courses in art. Enrollments in college, university, technical institute, and professional school art major courses are high and increasing. Yet in spite of this trend and the fact that many colleges require at least one art course of all students, high school art courses are rarely required of all students and are diffi-

---

[7] *Art Education for Scientist and Engineer* (Cambridge, Mass.: Massachusetts Institute of Technology, 1957), pp. 9, 10, and 11.

cult for bright students to elect because of excessive requirements in other subjects. Such courses are seldom recognized for college entrance credit and are therefore intentionally bypassed by many guidance counselors, who sometimes use them as time-fillers for "problem" students.

Because art courses are slighted in high schools, first-year college art courses often have to begin at a more elementary level than is desirable. The situation is rougly comparable to one in which youngsters would encounter their first study of literature as college freshmen, instead of taking courses based on four years of high school English. What should be a college-level course in which students develop a reasonably profound understanding of the visual and plastic arts can often be no more than a general introduction to the fields of painting and sculpture which most students could have successfully absorbed in junior or senior high school.

There are, unfortunately, many persons both in and out of the field of education—especially during the current stress on science and technology—who are little concerned about the exclusion of art education from most high school students' programs or the inadequacy of introductory art courses at the college level. In cases where these artistically ill-informed persons happen to be school board members, college trustees, educational administrators, conductors of school surveys, or writers of educational articles and books, much harm is done. Probably as much because of the inadequacy of their own art education as because of their desire to "improve" American education, these persons are being penny wise and pound foolish. A society made up of individuals who know little or nothing of the arts but who are highly trained in science and technology is likely to be as undesirable as those pictured in Orwell's *1984* and Huxley's *Brave New World*.

One might ask persons who would exclude the arts from the education of American youth: "What shall it profit a man if he shall gain the whole world but lose his own soul?" For the attainment of the *whole world* of scientific and technological superiority, many persons have apparently been willing to sacrifice the arts which are the *soul* of our culture.

Since only about fifteen per cent of college age youngsters now enter American institutions of higher learning and less than half of these successfully complete the four-year program, one might expect to be told that considerations of students' broad, consumer-type educational needs should be reserved for discussions of secondary school curricula. In terms of numbers of students, this is true; but in terms of the total educational needs of secondary school and college youngsters, it is false—indeed, it is harmful to the general welfare of our country and the world civilization of which it is a part.

College students—particularly those who go on to graduate—are destined for positions of leadership and responsibility in modern society. It is imperative that they be provided with art educational experiences of such scope and intensity that not only their personal lives but society as a whole will be aesthetically enriched. They must clearly understand the profoundly important role of art in community planning, architecture and interior design, education, industrial and commercial design, and the role of artistic expression in such fields as painting, sculpture, and the crafts. College students —many of whom will become leaders in business, industry, the professions, politics, religion, education, and community life— must be convinced of the human necessity of the arts. They must be helped to understand that a life devoid of art is not only barren and ugly, but psychologically and physically dangerous as well. Their education in the visual and plastic arts must make them determined to contribute to the aesthetic betterment of modern society. Their knowledge of the arts must bring them to a point where they will insist upon the highest possible aesthetic standards in all matters involving artistic judgment in their communities and homes and in the education of their children.

Courses in Art for Liberal Arts and Preprofessional Students

Programs of higher education in the liberal arts and preprofessional fields should include a minimum of two one-semester courses in art, each of which should meet for no less than four hours per week. Such courses should develop art knowledge and judgment rather than personal creative expression (except as the latter is necessary for developing insight into artists' media, techniques, and styles). Included in the two courses should be studies of historic and contemporary (with emphasis on the latter) painting, sculpture, architecture, community planning, graphic arts (including photography), industrial and commercial design, and crafts. Students should be made familiar with the aesthetic qualities of major examples in each art field and should, at the conclusion of the course, be able to make artistically sound value judgments on unfamiliar examples as well as on those to which they have previously been exposed.

Courses in Art for Elementary Education Students

The college education of elementary classroom teachers should include these same courses which should be related as closely as possible to other courses in the liberal arts and education. They should also take at least two additional courses: one in which they would learn to express themselves creatively in art media which could also be used by children; the other in the philosophy and methods of art teaching. In cases where classroom teachers are likely to be assigned to schools in which specially trained art teachers are not available, additional courses in the history of art, creative expression, and art educational philosophy and methodology should be required.

The Education of Art Teachers

It is now believed that the undergraduate and graduate education of art teachers should include a major sequence of courses in creative expression; a sizable number of art history courses; a few excellent courses in art (and general) educational philosophy, curriculum, methods, and student teaching; a major sequence of liberal arts courses; and a number of electives. Art education curricula developed in the past decade vary considerably, as indicated in Table 4.[8]

In a study of 280 universities, liberal arts colleges, teachers colleges, and professional schools, Kundis found the following re-

---

[8] Reported in Robert G. Beelke, "A Study of Certification Requirements for Teachers of Art in the United States," *Research in Art Education,* Yearbook of The National Art Education Association (Kutztown, Pa.: The Association, 1954), p. 55.

TABLE 4

VARIATIONS IN ART TEACHER EDUCATION CURRICULA *

	Credits Required
Studio Courses:	
Painting, sculpture, crafts, drawing design, graphic arts, photography, and so forth.	108–16
Art History Courses:	
Prehistoric, primitive, ancient, Middle Ages, Renaissance, modern.	13– 2
Art Education and Education Courses:	
Art educational philosophy, methods, curriculum, student teaching, and so forth; educational philosophy, educational psychology, history of education, general methods, general curriculum, and so forth.	47–16
Liberal Arts Courses:	
Philosophy, literature, music, foreign language, biology, physics, mathematics, history, sociology, anthropology, geography, speech and composition, and so forth.	74–16
Degrees Awarded: Bachelor of Fine Arts (B.F.A.), Bachelor of Arts (B.A. or A.B.), Bachelor of Science (B.S.), Bachelor of Science in Art Education (B.S.), Bachelor of Education (B.Ed.)	

* Based on a study of art education programs in thirty-three teachers colleges, twenty-three universities, and eight professional art schools.

quirements which, though they do not vary significantly from those presented by Beelke, represent a larger sampling and contain means as well as ranges in semester hours:

	Range	Mean
Graduation	120–190	125.9
Art	12–105	38.4
Art education	2– 32	5.1
Professional education (including student teaching)	6– 50	22.4
Student teaching	2– 15	16.4
	(70–675 hours)	(280 hours)
General studies	21– 74	47.7

The study also showed: . . . a mean requirement of 12.3 semester hours in free electives. These electives were used in the majority of institutions studied for additional work in the art field.[9]

---

[9] Lawrence Kundis, *Teacher Training Programs in Art Education in the United States*. Doctoral dissertation presented at the University of Southern California, **1954.**

More traditional curricula place a heavier emphasis on educational methods, student teaching, and pupil-oriented studio work. Those with a more contemporary orientation place greater stress on studio courses aimed at the development of personal artistic competence and on courses in art history and other liberal arts subjects in which it is not necessary to relate what is learned to teaching situations. The "contemporary" group does, however, highly value courses in art education which suggest effective means of teaching art but feels that such courses have often been too numerous, frequently repetitious, too broad in scope, too shallow in depth, and generally lacking in profundity, intensity, and value.

Typical four-year art education curricula in institutions of higher learning which have one or the other of the two following orientations might now require:

	CREDITS	
	Traditional Orientation	Contemporary Orientation
Studio courses	45	48
Art history courses	6	16
Art education and education courses	32	12
Liberal arts courses	45	54
Total	128	130

The five year B.F.A. degree programs now being offered by some universities and professional schools might require as much as seventy credits in studio courses; twenty-four in art history courses; forty in liberal arts courses, and twenty in electives (usually in art); as few as six in art education courses; and no education courses at all. But although these requirements are commendable and may indicate future trends in standard art education curricula, they disregard certification requirements in many states and thus automatically prevent their graduates (a surprising number of whom sooner or later go into part-time or full-time art teaching) from qualifying for art teachers' positions in public elementary and secondary schools. In most cases, persons holding the B.F.A. degree must take courses (usually as part of their work for a master's degree) in education and art education in order to secure an art teachers' license or certificate, although they may be hired on an emergency basis by school administrators who will then require them to complete all requirements except student teaching by taking in-service, evening, Saturday, or summer courses.

The Education of Professional Artists

Though there are still many persons, notably mature professional artists, who believe that artists cannot be formally trained, most would-be American artists today attend art schools, colleges, or universities where they take courses in drawing, painting, sculpture, architecture, community planning, design, the graphic arts, photography, art history, the liberal arts, and, sometimes, art education. Though some professional art schools still only require three years of study for a diploma, they are increasingly offering four-year degree programs (either independently or in conjunction with a college or university). The three-year programs are usually devoted exclusively to studio courses and art history; the four-year courses usually require additional work in the liberal arts and, for those who elect it, art education.

Unlike the art programs in most universities, liberal arts colleges, and colleges of education, professional art school curricula usually encourage students to major heavily in one art medium such as painting, sculpture, or the graphic arts. Professional art schools are also unique in offering curricula designed for the preparation of commercial artists and industrial designers. Their faculty members are usually practicing professional artists or designers who teach courses on a part-time basis. Standards for studio course work are often higher than those in colleges and universities.

Graduate Study in Art

Most colleges and universities, and some professional art schools, offer programs leading to the degree of Master of Art (M.A. or A.M.), Master of Fine Arts (M.F.A.), Master of Science (M.S.), Master of Science in Art Education (M.S.), or Master of Education (Ed.M.). Some universities offer graduate programs which lead to the Doctor of Philosophy (Ph.D.) or Doctor of Education (Ed.D.) degree. Except for the M.F.A. degree, graduate work in art usually requires students to take liberal arts courses as well as a major sequence of work in their area of special interest and, occasionally, a minor sequence in a related art area. A few universities have initiated doctoral programs in the creative arts, augmenting those which have existed for many years in art history and, more recently, in art education.

Graduate art students have considerable freedom to choose courses, even professors, within the scope of their interests. Their classes are usually smaller, fewer, and much more demanding than those on the undergraduate level. Seminars, tutorial study, and individual work in libraries, art studios, and museums and galleries, further intensify graduate study in art. It is the belief of many persons, both in and out of higher education, that the interdisciplinary nature of graduate study in art will have far-reaching and profound effects upon productivity and scholarship in the arts as well as upon modern civilization.

Though graduate degrees in both the study and practice of art are now generally looked upon with favor, those intended for painters, sculptors, and other practitioners were, until recently, looked upon with skepticism by practicing artists and others who felt that personally directed or apprentice-type training was more fruitful. But these people are coming to realize that the complexity of modern life, reflected in advanced art styles which seldom enjoy widespread communicability, can be better understood through skillfully taught, specifically oriented college courses than through the comparatively haphazard means of independent reading, informal conversation, and other day-to-day experiences. This realization, coupled with the understanding that an artist who expresses ideas based on a profound and extensive knowledge is more likely to achieve a high level of aesthetic significance than one who possesses mere technical facility, strongly suggests a college-level, integrated combination of studio work and academic study as the most logical means of educating artists.

Colleges, universities, and professional art schools are now seeking instructors who have earned graduate degrees in their fields of specialization—not only because of the value of a well-organized and intensive formal education, but also because presidents, deans, department chairmen, and accrediting associations prefer professors to hold degrees as high as (or higher than) the ones they grant to their students.

Summary

Art Education is basically comprised of two interrelated aspects: the creative, or expressive; and the aesthetic, or appreciative. Art education in the lower grades should stress creative expression and introduce children to appropriate examples of outstanding works of the visual and plastic arts. Formal or arbitrary standards of "right" and "wrong" should not be imposed on children at this stage; yet they should receive increasingly specific constructive criticism in both the development of their art expressive abilities and their aesthetic judgment. As they progress through the upper grades, secondary school, and college, individuals should receive art instruction in which aesthetically-oriented studies of major art forms occupy an increasingly larger portion of the curriculum. Such studies should be augmented by appropriate expressive activities, and supplemented by special studio classes for those who are especially interested or gifted.

The services of educationally prepared teachers of art, aided by art-informed classroom teachers and parents are held to be essential at all educational levels if the aims of modern art education are to be effectively realized.

CHAPTER VI

Art Education in the Community

Steadily growing enrollments in adult education and vastly improved mass communication have raised art (or what in many cases passes for art) to an unparalleled level of popularity. Courses in painting, the crafts, art appreciation, and related subjects abound in adult education programs. Programs on art are frequently presented on radio and television. Writings on art and reproductions of art works appear with increasing frequency in popular magazines as well as in professional publications. Reproductions of paintings and sculpture are now sold in department stores and bookstores. Exhibitions of paintings, sculpture, the graphic arts, photography, the crafts, and "good" design, as well as lectures and panel discussions, are presented by art galleries and museums throughout the country. Parent-teacher associations, libraries, and clubs sponsor sales of original art works, reproductions, art books, and art magazine subscriptions. Even billboards, newspapers, and popular magazines reproduce works of art. Popular magazines also occasionally offer parental advice on how to teach art to children, or offer how-to-do-it instruction in making art objects for the home.

On the basis of enrollments in adult classes, attendance at museums and galleries, sales of art books and reproductions, subscriptions to popular magazines as well as to art magazines, and numbers of listeners to and viewers of radio and television art programs, Americans would appear to be absorbing art at an unprecedented rate.

It must be acknowledged that many art books, reproductions of art works, museum exhibitions, and radio and television programs on art deal with legitimate art forms which are worthy of serious consideration. But persons who are familiar with even the most rudimentary principles of mass culture know that most persons who purchase art books, magazines, and reproductions, who tune in to radio or television programs on art, or who visit art galleries and museums are not really learning art or legitimate art educational procedures; and that most persons enrolled in adult education art classes and most of those who attend art lectures and panel discussions are not learning to produce works of artistic significance or to understand the aesthetic bases of what they see or hear.

Art is rarely understood at first glance or in capsule form: its frequent appearance in reproductions and magazine articles is not a guarantee of popular understanding. There is, in fact, evidence that the excessive (and usually faulty) presentation of reproductions and verbal analyses of art works diminishes their aesthetic impact. Concerning this, Margaret Mead states:

> It is said that the public has never been so "interested in art." This is only too true, and yet is this interest, expressed in the reproduction of objects never meant for reproduction and totally unrelated to their owners, a way of closing the gap between artist and critic and the common man, or of widening it? [10]

Art is one of man's most profound areas of productivity and scholarship. Its essence, though sometimes intuitively grasped, is usually understood only by persons who have applied themselves to its study with diligence, patience, and openmindedness. Ghiselin believes that even greater demands are made of the person who would understand the arts:

> "A work of art lives . . . through its suffusion with our inmost energies, which it allures into action, incites, sustains, and controls. That is, it does all this, or can do all this, if we give the work full attention and if we are competent to receive it, if our nervous systems have developed capacity to move in ways that the structure defines and facilitates, and if our minds are flexible and forceful enough in their action and pure enough in purpose and in desire of life to relinquish everything irrelevant to the experience offered and to concentrate upon it and in it." [11]

As indicated in Chapter I, art is infinitely more profound than the decorative or illustrative concepts prevalent among laymen. Art is seldom pretty, but it can be and often is beautiful. It is rarely true to life in appearance, yet it can provide us with much valuable in-

---

10 Margaret Mead, "Work, Leisure and Creativity," *Daedalus* (Winter, 1960), 20.
11 Brewster Ghiselin, "Cultivating Imagination," in *Education and the Imagination,* edited by Irving Kaufman (Ann Arbor, Mich.: University of Michigan Press, 1958), p. 20.

formation about the nature of things it interprets. It is, in a sense, indefinable, yet it is understood by many persons.

Most adult education art courses and mass communication media deal with art on the most superficial level imaginable. They attempt —almost always without success—to compress, to simplify, to make easily understandable a commodity of human genius which is, in its pure, whole, and original form, already as compressed, simple, and understandable as possible! Naively—or sometimes, one imagines, ruthlessly and crassly—adult educators and mass media personnel thus attempt to carry one step further what the world's most talented artistic geniuses and most intelligent scholars could not or would not do. Adult "art" educators, television "art" teachers, and publishers of how-to-do-it "art" books lead laymen to believe that anyone who will take a ten- or fifteen-session course, copy a step-by-step picture on the television screen, or buy a book can become an artist or learn to understand the arts. For the most part, the quality of art in adult education programs and the mass media is comparable to that of the medicine dispensed by eighteenth century peddlers.

Clearly, a major reversal of present attempts to educate the American public in art is now called for. Though innocence is no excuse, it must in fairness be said that until very recently art educational spokesmen and professional organizations neglected to comment on the quality of adult education art programs. Boards of education, administrators, and teachers responsible for programs of art education will, no doubt, soon be convinced of the importance of raising instructional levels and revising course length and content in the arts. By means of consultation, conferences, art teacher education, and contributions to professional literature, the growing number of art educators who sense the urgency of this situation must play an increasingly more active role in upgrading adult art education.

In a number of communities, adult art courses have already been improved. Individual courses are similar in scope, length, and instructional method to those in better high schools and colleges. Students must complete an introductory course before taking specialized work. Courses in the study of professional art forms are stressed as much as studio courses, and the areas of community planning, architecture, interior design, and the crafts have been added to the usual art history course coverage of painting and sculpture. Planned sequences of courses extending over a period of years are being made available, and aesthetically oriented creative teaching and working methods are stressed. Finally, evaluations of student progress are frequent and candid.

American art museums and galleries have long performed a highly creditable and vital cultural service by presenting thousands of outstanding exhibitions of the works of the world's artists. Many of these exhibitions have been augmented by useful catalogs with reproductions and explanatory texts. Most exhibitions have been, and continue to be, open to the public at little or no cost. A number of art museums have, in addition, developed educational programs which include classes for children and adults, gallery tours, lectures, forums, and demonstrations. Some institutions, such as the Cleveland Museum and New York's Metropolitan Museum of Art, have established direct connections with their respective city educational systems by means of which school children can receive a planned sequence of direct art learning experiences. New York's Museum of Modern Art has, under the leadership of noted art educator Victor D'Amico, developed its department of education to the point where it is a small but complete and outstanding art school for adults as well as for children of all ages.

But America needs many more art museums and galleries. Vast sections of the country have no art resources. Enlightened legislators are now developing plans which will enable the federal government to match funds allocated by states for the establishment of art museums. This legislation deserves the active support of all persons who are seriously concerned with America's culture. Nevertheless, present art museums must be encouraged and helped to extend their services by means of loan exhibitions to remote communities (some art museums have already established "artmobile" trailer trucks for this purpose, and New York State's Council on the Arts is financing traveling exhibitions), greatly extended and improved educational programs for children and adults, and a larger number and greater variety of higher quality exhibitions and publications, lectures, and forums. Direct relationships with public and private schools in the region should be established, by means of which certain original works [12] and reproductions could be borrowed, children could receive a planned sequence of guided tours, and special classes for teachers would better equip these persons for developing their pupils' understanding of the arts.

But the improvement of art education in the fields of mass communication media and business is quite another matter. A majority of the persons responsible for the production of commercial radio and television programs, art reproductions, how-to-do-it books, popular magazines, and numbered painting kits appear to be interested only in financial profit. One can only hope that:

1. They will voluntarily adjust to higher art educational standards, whether or not this adversely affects financial profit.

2. Ways might be found to raise mass media's art education standards without reducing financial profit.

3. Individual art educational spokesmen and professional groups will assume greater leadership in attempting to raise art educational standards in the mass communication media, and business. Professional organizations should, for example, establish criteria which would enable art teachers to endorse or condemn mass communication media and business ventures which contribute to or harm art education. Art teachers should be helped to understand the ethical necessity of openly stating their professional opinions on such matters, especially in light of the massive scale of these operations and their generally low aesthetic quality. Art teachers might, for example, send a letter to parents at the beginning of each school year, recommending particular radio and television programs, books, magazines, exhibitions, lectures, and special art classes in museums or community centers. Mention might also be made of certain programs, writings, or classes which are not recommended, though the mention of specific names would necessitate the presentation of adequate supporting data and, perhaps, the backing of a professional organization.

4. Local, state, and federal education and governmental agencies will assume responsibility for establishing minimal art educational standards for the mass communication media.

Perhaps the most fruitful of all efforts which culturally concerned individuals and groups might make would be the establishment of federal, state, and community art councils. Through these organizations, interested and capable persons in all walks of life would be able to achieve what individuals and smaller groups have been

---

[12] Many museums have vast collections of works in storage, at least some of which, if funds and proper security were provided, could be loaned to schools, colleges, and community centers.

unable to accomplish. The stunning success of New York State's recently established Council on the Arts provides adequate proof of the widespread high-level cultural benefits which can thus be attained. The accomplishments of the Council have already stimulated the establishment of local art councils in several other cities, and have caused federal legislators to study its professional and economic structure as a possible basis for establishing the eagerly awaited National Arts Council.

The passage of arts legislation on either the local, state, or federal level is difficult, to say the least. The public (and its elected governmental representatives) is reluctant to support something about which it knows little. Artistically enlightened individuals and groups will have to work long and hard (hopefully with the enthusiastic support of those few but important governmental leaders who understand the arts) in order to create governmental agencies which will aid art teachers, museums, and public-spirited citizens in making original works of art, educational programs in the arts, and the limitless values inherent in both readily available to all persons.

Summary

The art education of the child is influenced by many factors outside the school—through museums, films, television, and the adults with whom he comes into contact. Also, the importance of art education for the individual does not diminish upon his graduation from high school or college. Federal, state, and local programs of art education for adults are necessary in order that the adult members of the community may not only provide the proper background and atmosphere for encouraging art creativity in their children, but also in order that they may develop their own artistic ability and enhance their understanding and appreciation of art.

CHAPTER VII

Outlook for the Future of Art Education

We have seen that art is one of mankind's most important assets, but that its vast potential for bringing new and more profound meaning, greatly increased beauty, and happiness to human life has not yet been realized on a sufficiently broad basis. Emphasis has been given to the fact that modern civilization has an unparalleled opportunity to bring the arts into the lives of all human beings. It has also been pointed out that it is the teachers of art in elementary and secondary schools, colleges, and adult education programs who should be trained to assume primary responsibility for strengthening the arts in contemporary life.

A sizable number of art educators have begun to assume this responsibility. By refusing to be complacent about the present high level of professional productivity in the arts, by openly facing the fact that outstanding professional accomplishment is one thing and popular understanding quite another, and by suggesting specific means of giving children and adults an art education, they hope to gain the support of school officials, civic and governmental leaders, and enlightened private citizens. If the art education programs described in this volume can be implemented, the life of every child and adult will be profoundly benefited.

The notion that art is a frill, a luxury, something to be added to educational programs or private lives only if time and money permit must be replaced by the understanding that art is absolutely essential to human life, that it is as important to personal happiness and communal welfare as are science, technology, business, government, and other major fields of human endeavor, and that individuals and schools need not invest large amounts of money in order to enjoy art's many values. Persons responsible for structuring educational programs must be made to understand that art is as important as any of the basic school subjects. The accomplishment of this goal will require great effort and determination on the part of art educators, enlightened school officials, classroom teachers, guidance

101

counselors, educational theorists, and leaders in governmental and civic affairs.

The education of art teachers and the art education of classroom teachers, specialists in other subjects, future school administrators, and liberal arts students must be sharply upgraded in quality and scope. Certification requirements for art and classroom teachers must be adjusted accordingly. Both will necessitate major revisions in present curricula.

Art teachers, guidance counselors, classroom teachers, and parents will have to play active and sympathetic roles in the recruitment of future art teachers. Youngsters who appear to possess art ability and an interest in teaching should be actively encouraged to consider art teaching as a career. High school art teachers will need to provide apprentice teaching opportunities for such students.

To enable art teachers to develop the best possible art education programs in elementary and secondary schools, colleges, and adult education programs, school board members and administrators will have to provide adequate time, funds, and space. They will, in many cases, need to revise curricula to permit the inclusion of art as a required subject. They will particularly need to augment conventional art instructional materials with original art works (preferably owned by the school, but otherwise borrowed, rented, or seen as part of regularly scheduled field trips), slides, reproductions, and films. They will need to arrange schedules so art teachers will have time for preparation and evaluation between classes and are not burdened with routine assignments.

Institutions of higher learning will need to build art centers (many already have) in which adequate instructional programs as well as college art collections, slides, reproductions, and films can be housed. Art centers, as well as other college buildings, should be so designed that students may learn to understand significant architecture on a firsthand basis. Colleges and universities will need to appoint outstanding scholars and artist-teachers (many have already appointed artists-in-residence) who can meet the advanced needs of college students. College entrance requirements should allow credit for (and thus encourage enrollment in) high school art courses. Colleges will need to adjust their own requirements in such areas as the social sciences and literature in order that all students may be required to take at least one course in the visual arts.

Art museums and galleries will need to extend their exhibition, publication, and educational programs. The educational program must be enriched so that it is not merely a playful experience for children or a social event for dilettantes.

Local, state, and federal governments, private foundations, and businesses and industries must greatly increase their moral and financial support of the arts. They must realize that supporting the arts is more than a pleasurable charity. They must understand that the arts are, in fact, essential to modern civilization and that without a greater amount of moral and financial support the arts may really founder, and so may the civilization of which they are an integral part.

Governmental agencies can also serve the arts by working cooperatively with educators and artists to determine minimal art educational standards for the mass communication media and the marketing of such manufactured art products as self-instructional devices. Just as certain foods and drugs cannot be marketed because they are regarded as harmful by competent authorities, so, too, should products which flagrantly abuse widely accepted art educational theory be taken out of circulation. People's imaginations and emotions are no less worthy of serious attention than is their physical well-being.

Fortunately, many persons in positions of authority in the mass communication media—far from needing governmental and professional guidance in maintaining minimal educational and aesthetic standards—are able and willing to improve both the format and content of radio and television programs, popular magazines, newspapers, books, and such forms of advertising as billboards and store window displays. One finds increasing numbers of persons in both commercial and educational radio and television, publishing, and advertising who are trying to enlighten those of their colleagues who have not yet realized that they can and must strengthen, not merely reflect, our culture.

Among the accomplishments and plans of mass communication media leaders which deserve endorsement and expansion are:

1. Radio and television art programs of superb quality, involving distinguished artists and educators as advisors and performers, presented at desirable listening or viewing times and scheduled in the best interests of program content (i.e., two or more hours at one time, three one-hour

programs per week, one program a week for thirteen weeks, or the like). Distribution of supplemental literature, and the giving of high school or college credit for listeners and viewers who meet course requirements.

2. Statements by major artists, educators, and philosophers published in widely circulated popular magazines.

3. Subsidized publication of works of superb quality which, because of their present lack of popular appeal, would otherwise not reach the public.

Professional art and art education organizations must become much better organized and more forceful. Compared to organizations in other branches of the humanities and education, they have been ineffective. They have largely failed to communicate their professional beliefs and knowledge to members of other educational groups, to school administrators and boards of education, to government and foundation officials, and to the general public. They have, in fact, even failed to formulate a consensus on many professional matters. Professional art and art education organizations must reach agreement on fundamental beliefs and acceptable practices, state them in clear and convincing language, and communicate them to as many persons as possible. They must, particularly, make clear their beliefs on:

1. The essential role of the visual arts in American life and the need for art to be a required subject at all educational levels;

2. The need for special teachers of art in all elementary (primary as well as intermediate grades) and secondary schools;

3. The need for elementary school classroom teachers to augment, but not to replace, the instruction offered by specially prepared teachers of art;

4. The need for minimal educational standards for the preparation of elementary and secondary school art teachers, and for the art education of elementary school classroom teachers;

5. The need to stress aesthetically oriented creativity in pupils' art expression and to balance this aspect of art education with a broad, sequential study of professional art works;

6. The need for adequate time for programs of art education, and for enough time between classes for adequate cleanup, preparation, and evaluation;

7. The need to build collections of slides, films, reproductions, and original art works to supplement conventional art materials;

8. The need for new elementary and secondary school buildings to be outstanding examples of functional quality and aesthetic beauty which may be used for direct art instructional purposes;

9. The need for the government, foundations, and individual philanthropic donors to include the teaching of art as well as the professional practice of art, art exhibitions, and performances in their moral and financial support of cultural enrichment programs.

In their conferences, symposia, and publications, professional organizations in art and art education must involve representatives of educational administration, elementary education, the fine arts and other academic disciplines, government, and foundations. They must make a special effort to understand the problems of groups other than their own; they must take full cognizance of art's presently estranged role in many areas of human life, and attempt patiently and intelligently but persistently to attain mutual understanding.

Art educators, perhaps more than any other group in the arts, must recognize the uniqueness of their ability which, because of the breadth of their training in studio work, art history, art education, general educational theory, and liberal arts, qualifies them for the assumption of primary responsibility for strengthening contemporary culture. This is a tremendous responsibility, but who else can or will assume it? Artists are predominantly concerned with their own productivity. Art historians are frequently more interested in civilizations of the past than in contemporary affairs. General educators do not, as a rule, understand the importance of the arts. Specialists in the liberal arts are only rarely concerned with artistic regeneration. Though art teachers are busily occupied with day-to-day problems of teaching art to children, adolescents, college students, or adults, they must find time to speak and write about the need for art in the lives of all people. Having experienced art as creators, having learned about it and related liberal arts subjects as students, and having taught it to other people, art teachers are probably more aware of the total importance of art in human life than any other group of people. Their responsibility as outspoken advocates of cultural improvement will prove difficult and time-consuming. It will necessitate a revision in most of their current teaching and community activities. They will have to spend much more time in teaching students to understand their historical and contemporary artistic heritage and less time in fostering creative art expression. They will have to speak about art to parent-teachers associations and other community groups and to professional meetings of non-art groups; they will have to write for popular and professional magazines. Many of them will have to supplement their knowledge of the arts and related liberal arts subjects through independent reading, graduate study, and in-service training. But the time and effort they expend in so doing will not be wasted; indeed, without exaggeration, the cultural welfare of modern civilization may depend upon such effort.

One should not underestimate the power of effective and widely implemented art education; it could, within a generation, dramatically improve the quality of contemporary architecture, community planning, and industrial and interior design. If consumers are art educated to the point where they demand excellence in the design of homes, communities, and manufactured products, the persons responsible for producing them will be forced to upgrade their aesthetic quality. In similar fashion, art education could stimulate a public demand for superior aesthetic quality in painting, sculpture, and other art works.

Summary

We have made clear that neither America nor any other country is enjoying an artistic renaissance, published reports by popular culture enthusiasts to the contrary notwithstanding. As Gropius has said:

> Our modern society is still on trial where cultural integration is concerned. This certainly cannot be accomplished by handing out authoritative beauty formulas to an uncomprehending public, untrained to see, to perceive, to discriminate. A society such as ours which has conferred equal privileges on everybody will have to acknowledge its duty to activate the general responsiveness to spiritual and aesthetic values, to intensify the development of everybody's imaginative faculties. Only this can create the basis from which eventually the creative act of the artist can rise, not as an isolated phenomenon, ignored and rejected by the crowd, but firmly embedded in a network of public response and understanding.[1]

Modern man does, indeed, have the artistic resources, the ability, and the financial means to bring a cultural renaissance into being.

---

[1] Walter Gropius, in an address given upon his receipt of an honorary degree of Doctor of Humane Letters from Columbia University, March 21, 1961. Reported in *Arts and Architecture* (May, 1961), 28, 29.

We have suggested means by which such a highly desirable state of human affairs might be created. We can only fervently hope that persons of insight and ability will assume the responsibility necessary for the realization of this objective.

Bibliography

AESTHETICS AND CRITICISM

Arnheim, Rudolf, *Art and Visual Perception*. Berkeley, Calif.: University of California Press, 1954.

Dewey, John, *Art As Experience*. New York: Minton, Balch and Company, 1934.

Edman, Irwin, *Arts and the Man*. New York: W. W. Norton & Company, Inc., 1939.

Faure, Elie, *The Spirit of the Forms*. New York: Harper & Row, Publishers, 1930.

Focillon, Henri, *The Life of Forms in Art*. New Haven: Yale University Press, 1942.

Fry, Roger, *Vision and Design*. London: Chatto & Windus, Ltd., 1920.

Ghiselin, Brewster (Ed.), *The Creative Process: A Symposium*. Berkeley, Calif.: University of California Press, 1952.

Gombrich, E. H., *Art and Illusion*. New York: Pantheon Books, Inc., 1960.

Kepes, Gyorgy, *Language of Vision*. Chicago: P. Theobald & Company, Pubs., 1945.

Moholy-Nagy, Laszlo, *Vision in Motion*. Chicago: P. Theobald & Company, Pubs., 1947.

Munro, Thomas, *The Arts and Their Interrelations*. New York: The Liberal Arts Press, Inc., 1956.

ARCHITECTURE AND CITY PLANNING

Giedion, Siegfried, *Space, Time & Architecture*. 3rd ed. Cambridge, Mass.: Harvard University Press, 1954.

Hilberseimer, Ludwig, *The New Regional Pattern*. Chicago: P. Theobald & Company, Pubs., 1949.

————, *The Nature of Cities*. Chicago: P. Theobald & Company, Pubs., 1955.

Mumford, Lewis, *The Culture of Cities*. New York: Harcourt, Brace, & World, Inc., 1938.

Neutra, Richard, *Survival Through Design*. New York: Oxford University Press, Inc., 1954.

ART EDUCATION

Art for Elementary Schools: A Manual for Teaching. Curriculum Bulletin No. 2. New York: Board of Education of the City of New York, 1951–52.

Art in American Life and Education. Fortieth Yearbook of the National Society for the Study of Education. Bloomington, Ill.: Public School Publishing Co., 1941.

Barkan, Manuel, *A Foundation for Art Education.* New York: The Ronald Press Company, 1955.

Bland, Jane Cooper, *Art of the Young Child.* New York: The Museum of Modern Art, 1957.

Conant, Howard (Ed.), *Art Workshop Leaders Planning Guide.* Worcester, Mass.: Davis Publications, Inc., 1958.

Conant, Howard and Arne Randall, *Art in Education.* Peoria, Ill.: Chas. A. Bennett Co., Inc., 1963.

D'Amico, Victor, *Creative Teaching in Art.* Rev. ed. Scranton, Pa.: International Textbook Co., 1954.

de Francesco, Italo L., *Art Education, Its Means and Ends.* New York: Harper & Row, Publishers, 1957.

Fearing, Kelly, Clyde Martin, and Evelyn Beard, *Our Expanding Vision.* 8 vols. and teacher's manual. Austin, Texas: W. S. Benson & Co., 1960.

Gaitskell, C. D., *Art Education During Adolescence.* New York: Harcourt, Brace & World, Inc., 1954.

————, *Children and Their Art: Methods for the Elementary School.* New York: Harcourt, Brace & World, Inc., 1958.

Lindstrom, Miriam, *Children's Art.* Berkeley, Calif.: University of California Press, 1957.

Logan, Frederick M., *Growth of Art in American Schools.* New York: Harper & Row, Publishers, 1955.

Lowenfeld, Viktor, *Creative and Mental Growth.* 3rd ed. New York: The Macmillan Company, 1957.

McFee, June, *Preparation for Art.* San Francisco, Calif.: Wadsworth Publishing Co., Inc., 1961.

Mendelowitz, Daniel M., *Children Are Artists.* Stanford, Calif.: Stanford University Press, 1953.

Munro, Thomas, *Art Education: Its Philosophy and Psychology.* New York: The Liberal Arts Press, Inc., 1956.

National Art Education Association, *Yearbooks.* Kutztown, Pa.: The Association, 1950–present.

Progressive Education Association, Victor D'Amico, *et al.,* *The Visual Arts in General Education.* New York: Appleton-Century-Crofts, Inc., 1940.

Read, Herbert, *Education Through Art.* New York: Pantheon Books, Inc., 1945.

————, *The Grass Roots of Art.* New York: George Wittenborn, Inc., 1946.

Reed, Carl, *Early Adolescent Art Education.* Peoria, Ill.: Chas. A. Bennett Co., Inc., 1957.

Schultz, Harold A. and J. Harlan Shores, *Art in the Elementary School.* Urbana, Ill.: University of Illinois Press, 1952.

Wickiser, Ralph L., *An Introduction to Art Education.* Tarrytown, N.Y.: World Book Co., 1957.

Ziegfeld, Ernest, *Art in the College Program of General Education*. New York: Teachers College, Bureau of Publications, Columbia University, 1953.

DESIGN

Bassett, Kendall T. and Arthur B. Thurman, in collaboration with Victor D'Amico, *How to Make Objects With Wood*. New York: The Museum of Modern Art, 1951.

Duncan, Julia Hamlin and Victor D'Amico, *How to Make Pottery and Ceramic Sculpture*. Scranton, Pa.: International Textbook Co., 1947.

Kaufmann, Edgar, Jr., *What Is Modern Design*. New York: The Museum of Modern Art, 1950.

Lord, Lois, *Collage and Construction*. Worcester, Mass.: Davis Publications, Inc., 1958.

Mattil, Edward L., *Meaning in Crafts*. Englewood Cliffs, N.J.: Prentice-Hall, Inc., 1959.

Pollack, Peter, *Picture History of Photography*. New York: Harry N. Abrams, Inc., 1958.

Struppeck, Jules, *The Creation of Sculpture*. New York: Holt, Rinehart & Winston, Inc., 1952.

Winebrenner, D. Kenneth, *Jewelry Making As An Art Expression*. Scranton, Pa.: International Textbook Co., 1953.

HANDBOOKS AND PORTFOLIOS

Daniel, Greta (Ed.), *Useful Objects Today: Teaching Portfolio No. 4*. New York: The Museum of Modern Art, 1955.

d'Harnoncourt, Rene (Ed.), *Modern Art Old and New: Teaching Portfolio No. 3*. New York: The Museum of Modern Art, 1950.

Holden, Donald, *Art Career Guide*. New York: Watson-Guptill Publications, Inc., 1961.

DRAWING AND GRAPHIC ARTS

Albert, Calvin and Dorothy Seckler, *Figure Drawing Comes to Life*. New York: Reinhold Publishing Corp., 1957.

Heller, Jules, *Print Making Today*. New York: Holt, Rinehart & Winston, Inc., 1958.

Nicolaides, Kimon, *The Natural Way to Draw*. Boston: Houghton Mifflin Company, 1941.

HISTORIES OF ART

Barr, Alfred H., Jr. (Ed.), *Masters of Modern Art*. New York: The Museum of Modern Art, 1954.

Baur, John I. H. (Ed.), *New Art in America*. Greenwich, Conn.: New York Graphic Society, 1957.

Brion, Marcel, *et al.*, *Art Since 1945*. New York: Harry N. Abrams, Inc., 1958.

Gardner, Helen, *Art Through the Ages*. 4th ed. New York: Harcourt, Brace & World, Inc., 1958.

Gombrich, E. H., *The Story of Art*. 6th ed. New York: Phaidon Publishers, Inc., 1954.

Janson, H. W., *History of Art*. Englewood Cliffs, N.J. and New York: Prentice-Hall, Inc., and Harry N. Abrams, Inc., 1962.

McCurdy, Charles (Ed.), *Modern Art: A Pictorial Anthology*. New York: The Macmillan Company, 1958.

HISTORIES OF PAINTING

Barr, Alfred H., Jr., *What Is Modern Painting*. Rev. ed. New York: The Museum of Modern Art, 1956.

Haftmann, Werner, *Painting in the Twentieth Century*. 2 vols. New York: Frederick A. Praeger, Inc., 1960.

Index

113